THE
DOG OWNER'S
HANDBOOK

THIS IS A CARLTON BOOK

Design and commissioned photographs
copyright © 2002 Carlton Books Limited
Text copyright © Annette Conn

This edition published in 2010 by
Carlton Books Limited
20 Mortimer Street
London W1T 3JW

ISBN 978 1 84732 731 4

Printed and bound in Dubai

Editorial Manager: Judith More
Executive Editor: Zia Mattocks
Senior Art Editor: Barbara Zuñiga
Editors: Siobhán O'Connor & Sian Parkhouse
Designer: Zoë Dissell
Picture Editor: Elena Goodinson
Production: Kate Pimm
Art Director: Penny Stock

The author and publisher have made every
effort to ensure that all information is
correct and up to date at the time of
publication. The behaviour of dogs is
beyond the control of the author and the
publisher, neither of whom can accept
responsibility for any accident, injury or
damage that results from using the ideas,
information or advice offered in this book.

THE
DOG OWNER'S
HANDBOOK

The Complete Guide to Choosing, Rearing and Training

Annette Conn

CARLTON
BOOKS

contents

introduction

Whether you're thinking of buying a dog or are already a dog owner, this book tells you what you really need to know and answers the most commonly asked questions. Even experienced dog owners should find the advice given here useful. Dogs have different personalities and needs, even within the same breed, and your experience with one dog does not always prepare you for your next one. If only I had a penny for every time I've heard the phrase 'I've had dogs all my life, but I've never had one like this before!', I'd be a very rich woman...

The advice in this book is born out of the experiences, successes and mistakes of the many dog owners I have encountered over the years. A great number of them learnt the hard way that, however optimistic and full of good intentions they were, love and kindness on their own were not enough to raise a happy, healthy, well-behaved pet. Dogs have a very specific set of needs, which, if neglected, can adversely affect their – and your – quality of life; you'll want to get it right for your own sake, as well as for your dog's.

Behaviour and training problems are the number one reason that dogs are abandoned, found new homes or destroyed. Most of these dogs are not intrinsically bad, but were given a poor start in life because their owners failed to rear them properly or provide adequately for their needs. Many of these behaviour problems are common ones that could easily have been avoided if only the owners had been armed with the right information from the start. Most of the dog owners I have helped over the years were unaware that things were going wrong until there was a problem that couldn't be ignored. Once they understood the reason and learnt how to meet their dog's needs, and manage them better, the problems diminished and often completely disappeared.

Choosing the right dog is the first and most important step to ensuring that your relationship with your faithful friend is a mutually beneficial and contented one. This starts with choosing a breed that best suits you and your circumstances. Remember that looks and size are much less important than breed type and predisposition. Consider what job your intended dog was bred to do and whether you are prepared to cope with the associated patterns of behaviour that come with it. Is it an energetic terrier you're after or do you want a quieter breed that was bred for companionship? Where you buy your dog is also hugely important – the information in Choosing the Right Dog (page 10) will point you in the right direction. This is one time when background and breeding are key.

Bringing your puppy home and settling it in can be made much easier with a bit of preparation. It is vital that things go right from the start, yet many owners make common mistakes that are harder to rectify later on than if they are nipped in the bud. Puppy Love (page 24) provides guidelines for giving your dog the best possible start in its new home.

It also helps to be aware that most puppies and dogs will test you and your boundaries. In fact, they can act like hooligans if you let them. Teaching Good Manners (page 42) details how to train your pooch from the outset, and this will help you avoid common problems. If you encourage perfect canine etiquette, your dog will become a pleasure, not a pain.

Caring for your new dog doesn't stop with toilet training and providing regular food and water and a warm, dry bed. Dogs also need to be taught to understand simple commands, and this is where Basic Training (page 56) comes in. It deals with how to teach your dog to sit down, stand, stay and come to you when it is called. Once you have mastered these basics, it is time to move on. Lots of dogs pull on their leads and are boisterous, so Further Training (page 70) outlines how to teach your dog to walk beside you, rather than dragging you at arm's length, and also to settle down, so that it is the perfect picture of obedience wherever you may be.

Walkies! (page 82) addresses the question of exercise: how much, how often, where and when. All dogs need regular, free-running exercise and the chance to mix with other dogs, and this chapter helps you to achieve this.

Adolescence can be as trying for canines as it is for humans; hormonal changes can drastically alter your dog's character. Puberty and Sexual Behaviour (page 90) tells you what to expect, how to handle it and whether to neuter your dog.

Keeping your dog regularly fed and watered becomes so habitual you do it without thinking, but not without care and thought as to the type and amount of food. The old saying that 'you are what you eat' is just as applicable to your dog. What and how you feed your dog can have a huge effect on its health, temperament and development, so read A Dog's Dinner (page 98) for the dos and don'ts of doggie diets.

Grooming is also essential to keep your dog in the peak of health. Good Grooming (page 106) tells you what you need to do to keep your dog looking the sleekest hound on the block, and teaches you how to check for any health problems.

Accessorizing is everything. You can spend a small fortune on canine accoutrements, with everything from designer clothes and toys to custom-made beds and kennels available. Shop Till You Drop (page 114) tells you what you really need to buy and what is merely a waste of your hard-earned cash.

Once you have acquired your bundle of joy and have learnt how best to raise and train it, keep it fit and healthy, and ensure that it has all its material wants satisfied, then you need to know what to do if anything should go wrong and how to deal with any glitches along the way. Avoiding Bad Behaviour (page 124) highlights common problems and explains how to negotiate them. And for all those day-to-day concerns, from how to stop your dog stealing your favourite slippers to what to do with a fussy eater, turn to Frequently Asked Questions (page 132).

Remember, owning a dog should be about joy and reward for you and your faithful companion. Ensuring that you both receive the benefits while avoiding the pitfalls really is up to you — it just takes a little planning, time, responsibility and love. Here's to a long, happy and rewarding relationship.

CHOOSING THE RIGHT DOG

They say that a dog is man's best friend – and woman's, too – and that owning a dog can be good for your health, as it can reduce your blood pressure, make you take more exercise and provide you with love and companionship. If it's true that people with pets live longer, your new pooch is going to be there to help you while away the hours as you reap the benefits. If you purchase the wrong type of dog or live in the wrong environment, however, the opposite can be true. It is then that the dream of pet ownership can rapidly turn into a nightmare.

Choosing the right dog is vital to both your wellbeing and your sanity – and to your dog's, so there are several things you need to bear in mind before you rush off to purchase that bundle of joy.

BEFORE YOU DECIDE TO BUY A DOG, READ ON ...

The rewards of dog ownership are great, but the costs should also be considered – pragmatically. You need to make sure that you, as the optimistic owner, do not have unrealistic expectations. Otherwise it will be not only you but also your confused and possibly spoiled dog that will pay the price – and that is simply unfair.

DOGS CAN BE EXPENSIVE

They can cost a lot to buy, and initial start-up costs can be high. Purchase price, veterinary inspection, worming, vaccinations, a puppy pen, a crate or child gates, insurance, bedding, toys, collars, leads, books and grooming equipment – the list goes on. You may also need to re-fence your garden or yard. And then there are those unexpected costs, such as repairing any damage to your home, car or garden that your dog might surprise you with.

Dogs also cost a lot to run. For example, there are food bills, worm and flea control, training classes, veterinary bills, boarding fees, visits to the grooming parlour and professional dog walkers.

DOGS CAN BE INCONVENIENT

All dogs need to be fed, watered and exercised regularly. Just because you've had a bad day at work, it doesn't mean that you can neglect supplying these basic needs. Puppies need to be taken outside every hour or two for the first few months. It isn't good enough to take a couple of weeks off work and hope to cram several months' worth of toilet training into such a short time.

Even adult dogs need attention. They need room to run around and, if they do not have access to the outdoors, they need to be taken out every few hours. Many owners cannot leave the house for more than a few hours at a time unless they employ a dog sitter or walker – and these can be expensive or even unsuitable.

Then there is the question of holidays. There will be no more last-minute weekends away or two-week vacations in the sun without planning what you will do with your dog while you are away.

Above Do you have what it takes to give a dog a good home? You need to think about this carefully.

DOGS ARE SOCIAL ANIMALS

Dogs like company as much as the next party animal. Many dogs can become stressed when they are left on their own in a house or garden for extended periods, and they will often resort to noisy or even destructive behaviour as a result. Some owners do leave their dogs on their own all day, but for each one that manages it successfully, there are many more that don't. You shouldn't even consider getting a puppy or an older dog if you are going to leave it alone while you are at work all day. It is unfair – all dogs need companionship.

DOGS CAN BECOME A PROBLEM

Life – and dog ownership – does not always run smoothly, and many dog owners experience problems for a variety of reasons. Some people get the help they need to work through this, but there are also tens of thousands of dogs abandoned each year by initially well-intentioned owners. Sadly, it is the dog that pays the highest price for its owner's naivety. A few lucky ones might find a new home, but the stark reality is that the vast majority of these 'once-loved' pets will end up being needlessly destroyed. You need to be realistic about your circumstances and your expectations BEFORE you take on the responsibility of a dog.

HAVING A DOG IS HUGELY TIME-CONSUMING

Puppies are a full-time job and are very high maintenance. They need a great deal of routine care, training, supervision and company, especially in the early months. Parents frequently comment that having a puppy is like looking after a newborn baby all over again. Don't kid yourself that your children (if you have them) will do most of the work – no matter what they promise, they rarely deliver in the long term.

Adult dogs can also be a lot of work. They need companionship and a decent free run in the park every day (come rain, hail, sleet, snow or shine). They need to be cleaned and dried when they are muddy, groomed regularly and properly trained. They are also quite high maintenance for the first year or so (or longer if you are unlucky or have neglected your early training). Some dogs are high maintenance for their entire lives.

YOUR HOME WILL NEED A LOT OF EXTRA CLEANING

It's not just the hair, so don't think a non-shedding breed is the answer. It's also the mud. Say goodbye to stylish light-coloured carpets and neat and tidy furnishings, and hello to sofa throws, washable rugs and dog toys strewn everywhere.

DOGS ARE A LIABILITY

Owning a dog brings with it many responsibilities – not just the basic ones of food, water and shelter. For instance, as its owner, you can be held legally liable for any damage that your dog causes to a person or their property, so it is important to know where you stand if the worst should happen. You may also need to consider special restrictions that apply to certain breeds of dog, such as some bull terriers, and whether the breed that you want is allowed where you live.

DOG OWNERSHIP CAN BE A CHALLENGE

Your visions of the perfectly groomed, perfectly behaved pooch as the ultimate fashion accessory should be nipped in the bud right now. Your dog may well test your boundaries, particularly during its adolescence. If you behave like a doormat, it will probably take great delight in walking all over you. It may endeavour to manipulate you with attention-seeking behaviour such as stealing, jumping up or play biting. It will probably jump on your guests, chase and 'playbite' the children, pull on its lead and ignore your instructions unless it suits them. That is, unless you teach your dog otherwise, which takes quite a bit of work and planning.

MAKING THE RIGHT CHOICE

Choosing the right dog is one of the most important decisions you are ever likely to make. Incredibly, most people put more thought into choosing a washing machine than buying a dog, but your choice of dog will influence your life far more than your washing machine ever will. Dogs can change our lives considerably, and they are a long-term commitment. Most problems stem from not choosing a dog that best suits your circumstances. Do not be influenced by looks, tempting though that may be. Remember that beauty is only skin deep, and some of the cutest-looking breeds can also be the most inappropriate.

Below Research thoroughly a breed's traits, temperament and potential health problems before you make your decision.

PAWS FOR THOUGHT
Before you even begin to choose a puppy or older dog:
● Speak to several reputable local dog trainers for sound advice on what breed might suit you best.
● Find a vet – by recommendation if possible – and check out the facilities. Ask the vet's opinion about the type of dog you should get, any potential health problems and the best insurance company for settling claims.
● Start researching where and when you can find your new puppy or dog.

SO WHAT IS A SUITABLE DOG?

The answer to this question all depends on your home circumstances and what you want from your dog. Do you have room for a large, active dog, one that you can take jogging with you around the park? Or are you looking for a smaller companion with a quieter nature? Is your canine friend going to be part of a boisterous family or an addition to a household of one?

All the different types of breed were evolved to fulfil specific and specialized roles and they have a predisposition to certain behaviours. Generally speaking, these are the factors you need to consider when choosing a suitable pet (though there are exceptions to every rule):

Working and utility dogs perform a variety of very different jobs, so check your intended breed beforehand to find out exactly what you can hope to expect from your dog. Boxers, Great Danes, Dalmatians, poodles and English bulldogs all fall into this category.

Crossbreeds and mongrels often display a mixture of their ancestor's traits, so it is important to take this into account.

Right There is more to choosing a breed than size alone.

Toy dogs such as pugs, papillons and Cavalier King Charles spaniels can make excellent pets. Problems arise when they are treated like babies or toys. Don't be misled by their name and small size – even a toy dog, such as a Yorkshire terrier (below), is 100 percent dog and should be treated as such.

Hounds hunt or track by sight or scent. These instincts are so strong that they can be very difficult to train and control. Hounds have also been bred for speed or endurance, and their ability to catch (and dispatch) their prey. Breeds of hound include beagle, bassett, dachshund and greyhound.

Pastoral dogs herd and guard, so German shepherds and collies (above) are much more likely to chase and nip joggers, cats, kids and cars. They can also be overprotective and difficult to control, so unless you are prepared to put a lot of time and effort into training, and keep them fully occupied, they might not suit you. These dogs need to be properly exercised every day, so will not suit couch potatoes. German shepherds, collies, briards, corgis and Old English sheepdogs are included among this type.

Terriers are tough, active, busy dogs. Bred to dig, catch and often kill various other animals, they can be excitable and feisty. Quick to react and sometimes very noisy, they may not suit families with small children or other pets, or people who live in flats or apartments. They include Jack Russell, Scottish (right) and Border terriers.

Gundogs were bred to find, pick up and carry game birds, which is why so many will greet you with a slipper or a cushion in their mouth. While this can be an endearing trait, the downside is that they can be dreadful scavengers. They also love water and muddy puddles. Retrievers (above), setters and spaniels are all gundogs.

WHAT ELSE SHOULD I CONSIDER?

Will the size of your chosen dog suit your home, car, children and exercise plans? What about friends or family who may look after it when you are away on holidays? Large dogs normally have a much shorter life span than smaller dogs and they can cost more to feed. Their veterinary treatment and insurance normally cost more, too.

What about coat type and length? Will you mind spending hours grooming and cleaning your dog (and your house), or do you want a low-maintenance breed? Some breeds have a strong smell; others dribble a great deal. Do you think you can you live with these characteristics?

Buying two dogs together is a bad idea. While they may keep each other company, they will do so at the cost of your relationship with them. Rearing two puppies successfully takes an enormous amount of work, as you have to rear them separately and give each individual quality time, space, exercise and training. This prospect is definitely not for the faint-hearted or busy dog owner.

If you already have a dog and would like a companion for it, bear in mind that many dogs prefer being the only dog in the family and will resent another moving in

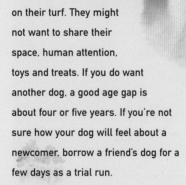

on their turf. They might not want to share their space, human attention, toys and treats. If you do want another dog, a good age gap is about four or five years. If you're not sure how your dog will feel about a newcomer, borrow a friend's dog for a few days as a trial run.

HEALTH

All breeds have potential health problems (with eyes, joints, heart, or hearing, for example), and many breed clubs have excellent screening programmes to help you minimize the chance of buying a dog with hereditary defects. Contact the breed

Right Not all dogs are easy to own, particularly the strong ones. Think about the space you have and the space your new dog will need.

Above Always view the puppy with
its mother before making your
decision. If you can't, don't buy it.

TEMPERAMENT

Some dogs are bred for looks, others for their working ability – the result is that there is a whole range of temperaments in between. The right one for you depends on many variables, so seek expert help on your intended breed and be very careful about where you purchase your puppy.

Never buy a puppy without seeing its mother with it (see the section on dealers on page 20). Do not believe any excuses about why the mother is not available for viewing. Make sure that the mother has a good temperament, as she sets an important example for the puppy to follow. Mothers should not mind you looking at their puppies, so don't buy one if the mother is nervous or aggressive.

Whether you would be better with a male or female, or a puppy or an adult dog, depends on many considerations. Discuss your options with a couple of experienced dog trainers, your prospective veterinary surgeon, potential breeders (who will be informative, but who may also be wearing rose-tinted glasses when it comes to their own breed) and rescue organizations (who are normally grittily realistic). These people will be happy to share their experiences and views with you, and they should give you a good range of opinions to consider.

club of the dog you are interested in (you can get their details from the Kennel Club or on the Internet), and they will tell you most of what you need to know. Bear in mind that you will probably be talking to someone with a distinct bias, so always confirm any information with your vet or dog trainer. If the puppies or parents have been screened for defects, always ask for copies of the certificates. The breeder should be happy to give them to you. Don't be polite and assume that what they tell you is true, as, unfortunately, many people are hoodwinked this way.

Left Ask to see a copy of the dog's pedigree and any health certificates before you buy.

REPUTABLE BREEDERS

Find a responsible and recommended breeder via the breed clubs, the details of which you can get from the Kennel Club or the Internet. Try to purchase a dog from a breeder who has their dogs living in their home, as opposed to living in kennels. This shows that the animals can coexist with humans, whereas their kennelled counterparts are much more of an unknown quantity.

Experienced breeders may be able to give you help and advice, but they can also be a little set in their ways, so take that into account. Always keep in mind that you are talking to someone who is biased towards a particular breed – you need to check their advice with another source.

Visit several litters before you decide, so that you have something to compare before making your choice. The ideal age to buy is between seven and eight weeks old. Do not pick the first puppy that you see, and don't buy the shy puppy or the boldest – although this can change daily. It is best to see the puppy at least a couple of times before deciding to buy it.

Ask for a copy of the pedigree, and look for any inbreeding (brother-to-sister or father-to-daughter matings) or close line-breeding (uncle-to-niece mating). Keep an eye out for the same or similar names cropping up, and don't buy the pup if its parents are too closely related. Get a second opinion if you are unsure.

EX-BREEDING DAMS

Breeders sometimes sell off bitches when they are barren or too old for breeding. These dogs are often institutionalized, especially if they have spent their lives in kennels, so be aware of this.

> PAWS FOR THOUGHT
>
> Consider how old a puppy is before you make a decision. It may not be wise to buy an older puppy (one that is older than 10 weeks) which has been kept back by the breeder as a potential show dog or as surplus stock, or has been returned to the breeder. Often these puppies have problems. If they have remained with the breeder's other dogs, they tend to adapt less well to living on their own than they would have at seven or eight weeks of age. They are also often undersocialized. However, if the breeder can show you that it has been well socialized – it is not timid of traffic, being in a car or with dogs other than its own family – and is happy to be separated from its family, it may be worth considering. Only purchase it on the condition that if it is unhappy or nervous, you can return it for a refund.

RESCUE KENNELS AND OTHER RESCUE ORGANIZATIONS

Consider giving a home to a dog from an animal shelter or rescue organization if you are prepared to put in the extra work that may be needed. Do not consider this, however, if you have a busy life or young children, as these dogs often need special care. Find out as much as you can about the dog, as this may help you to settle it in. If your chosen dog doesn't have a confirmed case history, make sure that you can return it if it doesn't fit into your household. Ex-racing greyhounds usually make excellent pets, but may not if you have cats or other animals.

PUPPY FARMS, DEALERS AND PET STORES

Puppy farms are similar to factory farms, where dogs live intensively like battery chickens and are bred purely for profit. The dogs are normally overbred, unhealthy and live in unbearably poor conditions. Puppies are often removed from their mothers far too early and sent in overcrowded cages to 'dealers' or pet stores to satisfy public demand. Many are severely traumatized by the transition, and some do not survive the journey. Do not buy a dog from these sources, as they will have had the worst possible start in life, and they are far more likely to have health and temperament problems.

Lots of 'puppy farm' puppies come with proper pedigrees and Kennel Club registration, but this is NOT an indication of quality. Pedigrees are relatively easy to fake, so they are often not worth the paper they're written on, and Kennel Club registration simply means a puppy's name was registered with the Kennel Club's database – there is no guarantee it will be in good condition or well bred.

'Dealers' are agents for puppy farms. They buy their stock and advertise them in newspapers and magazines, sometimes masquerading as breeders. If an ad has more than one breed of puppy for sale, it has most likely (although not always) been placed by a dealer. You should always be able to view the mother with the puppies, so ask them if you can do this. If you can't see the mother, or if they make some excuse, such as she was tired of the litter and is with a relative, do not buy a puppy from them. NEVER buy a dog from the back of a car or at a motorway service station, as this is how many dealers operate. NEVER buy a puppy or dog from a pet store – it probably originated from a puppy farm. Good breeders would never sell their puppies via a pet store or an intermediary.

CHILDREN AND DOGS

Buying a puppy or dog for your children and expecting that they will look after it is a Utopia that rarely exists. In real life, this notion is neither practical nor realistic, and all too often it's the dog that pays the price for the family's optimism.

People often choose dogs or puppies that grow up to be too large or strong for their children to control. The reality is that most dogs are capable of taking off after another dog, a cat or a bird and pulling an unsuspecting child into the path of traffic, so it is not worth taking the chance. If you're uncertain, borrow a similar type and size of dog from a friend or breeder, and test the strength of the dog – and your child – in your garden or backyard. Give your child the lead – with dog attached, of course – and ask the owner to call the dog back to them enthusiastically. If the child cannot hold the dog back and releases the lead or is pulled along, you definitely need to reconsider your choice of dog.

Puppies play by chasing after and jumping on fast-moving objects and biting them with their needle-sharp puppy teeth. If your child is too young to understand

and be able to cope with these painful but accidental nips, it is better to wait until he or she is older before getting a dog.

Even older kids are excitable and inconsistent in their behaviour, so it can be almost impossible to stop children from encouraging the dog one minute and then telling it off (and often smacking it) the next. Children are not known for their patience, so they can be very difficult to have around a puppy or new dog.

Generally speaking, eight years old is a good minimum child's age for getting a dog or a puppy, but this rule of thumb depends on the maturity of the child.

Are your children old enough to go to the park on their own or to take the dog out after dark? If they aren't, remember that you will still have to accompany them or go in their place.

Do your children have really hectic schedules with lots of after-school activities and homework? Are you forever ferrying them here and there? If so, when are they (or you) going to find the time to socialize, train and exercise the dog?

Who will look after the dog while the children are at school and you are at work? It is unreasonable to expect the au pair, nanny or neighbour to be sufficiently committed to undertake the task, so this sort of arrangement consistently fails.

Children may promise you anything in order to persuade you to get a puppy, then lose interest as soon as the novelty wears off. Just think of all those expensive toys and games they simply had to have that are now gathering dust in a cupboard somewhere. Only make the decision to own a dog on the basis that you are prepared to take complete care of its needs yourself.

Left Puppies chew toys and clothes. Minimize their opportunity to do this in order to avoid mishaps.

All too commonly, pups are routinely overstimulated into hyperactive behaviour by the children in their household, which can easily progress to becoming overly boisterous with visiting kids, too. This doesn't just occur in the house, but also in the park when they chase after and jump all over other people's children. Not surprisingly, this upsets both the parents and the children, so you should curtail any wild behaviour at home to prevent this happening when you are out and about, and want your dog to be the epitome of well-trained courtesy.

Do your children understand that the dog is not a toy or doll, and cannot be picked up, cuddled, kissed, carried around or dressed up? A dog is not a plaything, and most dogs dislike close face-to-face contact unless they themselves have instigated it. Breaking this rule can often mean that they end up being snappy or aggressive, so be prepared to insist on this point until it is understood.

Are your children messy or untidy? Dogs will often steal, chew and swallow children's toys and clothes for attention, so teach your little darlings tidy habits well before you agree to get a puppy or it will spend its youth at the vet's surgery having things surgically removed from its gut. Or worse – it could die.

Your dog's trustworthiness will depend a great deal on how your (and other people's) children are allowed to interact with it. You must bear in mind that NO dog is completely predictable with children, not least because children themselves can be unpredictable and unwittingly frightening at times. Dogs can easily misread this.

Never let children ambush your dog or force themselves on it. If they want to fuss over the dog, they should be invited over, but do not let them force the issue if the dog does not want to go. Children must be made to understand the importance of leaving the dog alone and giving it peace when it wants some.

Children can't be trusted to behave appropriately at all times. They should only be allowed to interact with the dog under supervision. Children love teasing dogs, which encourages bad behaviour, and dogs dominate children quite easily.

Children (and adults) who have a dog at home are sometimes overconfident with other people's dogs, so make a special effort to teach your children (and their friends) not to approach strange dogs without the owner's permission. Make sure that they know to offer their hand palm uppermost to dogs (rather like feeding a horse). They should also never pass their hands over a dog's head as an initial greeting, and they must be taught to realize that many dogs hate being patted on the top of the head.

Below Children and dogs can work well together if they are properly supervised and given consistent boundaries, training and patience.

2 PUPPY LOVE

Once you have found your ideal companion, you need to prepare your puppy, yourselves and your home for the new arrival. The journey home can be quite traumatic for your puppy, and the first few weeks in its new abode can be disorientating and confusing. You should do all you can to minimize this. Good planning and preparation can help you to avoid most of the common mistakes, and give your household and the puppy the best possible start.

There are several things you must do
before bringing your puppy or dog home.

- Make your garden dogproof, and
section off part of your kitchen or install
a child gate in the doorway to the rest
of the house.
- If you have children, make a contract
with them about their responsibilities,
chores and behaviour around the puppy.
- Work out a roster with the household
for toilet and basic training.
- Choose an insurance company to
cover the costs of veterinary treatment
in case your precious pup becomes ill,
and for third-party liability insurance to
cover you against any claims for
damage that your dog may cause.

Above Successful puppy rearing
requires a bit of forward planning
and preparation.

PREPARING YOUR HOME

Make ready a safe, contained area where
the puppy will sleep and spend most of
its unsupervised time. This area should
have easy access to your garden or yard.
Most people find that their kitchen makes
an ideal puppy nursery and crèche. The
puppy should not be allowed access to the
other rooms until much later, when it has
better bladder and bowel control.

A cardboard box with all the staples
removed is an ideal solution for your
puppy's first bed – anything better will
simply be chewed. Do not use a wicker
basket for a pup, as it can hurt itself if it
chews it. Plastic oval beds are good, but
you need one big enough for your pup to
stretch out in when it is fully grown, as
not all dogs like to curl up.

The bed should be placed in a warm,
draught-free area, which needs to be
securely fenced off to prevent the puppy
from getting underfoot when you are
busy. You can section off a small area
of a room by using a child gate or buy
a proper puppy pen – it's up to you.

COLLECTING YOUR NEW DOG

Take a large empty water bottle with you
so that you can bring back some of the
water the puppy is familiar with to use for
the first few days. This helps to avoid the
added disruption of stomach upsets at
the most critical time. After a few days,
you can start mixing in your own water,
so that the changeover is a gradual one.

For the same reason, bring some of
the breeder's food home with you to feed
to the puppy or dog for the first few days.

If you intend to change the diet, do so a few days after your pup has settled in. The new diet should be introduced gradually over a period of several days.

THE JOURNEY

Take a spacious cardboard box or travel crate, and line it with newspaper and blankets to provide comfort on the journey home. This set-up is much better for the puppy than being forcefully restrained on someone's lap or being free to wander around the vehicle with the risk of falling and injuring itself. Someone can put their hand close to the dog for company, but they should try not to pick it up and cuddle it, especially if is distressed or car sick. This may only unwittingly teach the dog to be apprehensive of close contact with them.

Make sure the dog isn't fed before you collect it, as the journey home can be made worse by travel sickness. Also, puppies that have endured a traumatic journey are far more difficult to 'car train' later. This problem is commonly seen in pups that originate from puppy farms far away from their dealers or pet stores. Puppies from good breeders may have already been introduced to car travel, so should mind significantly less!

Ask the breeder to put a cloth (an old T-shirt will do) in the pup's bedding. This allows it to absorb the familiar, comforting scent of 'home'. Bring this 'comfort cloth' home with you and use it in the car and in the puppy's bed to help it settle in during the first few days.

If your puppy should become sick or distressed during the journey home, remove the cloth – otherwise you will only have to wash it, which will remove all its nice, familiar smells and hence defeat its purpose. When you arrive home, put the comfort cloth in your puppy's new bed straight away. If you are acquiring an older dog, it may help to bring home a jumper or sweater smelling of its previous owner for the same reason.

Below There is no need to go overboard – a cardboard box and blanket make an ideal first bed.

WHEN YOU GET HOME

Take the puppy straight out into your garden or yard to allow it to urinate or defecate. When it is finished, you should put it into its pen so it can recover its bearings after the journey. Put the '

comfort cloth' and some chew toys in its bed and pour some of its water into a bowl. Give it ten minutes to check out its new environment with as little interference from you as possible.

Don't take the puppy anywhere other than its penned-off area and the garden or yard at this stage. Taking it into other rooms will confuse it and allow it a chance to go to the toilet in the wrong place.

Keep impatient children and adults away. Your new puppy is likely to be disorientated and possibly even scared, so it needs a bit of space and time to adjust. Do not pick up or carry the puppy around (except when necessary).

Don't be tempted to cuddle your puppy and 'mollycoddle' it. This will just make it clingy, and you'll have problems getting it to bed on its own later. It may

also lead to you having to spend the first few nights sleeping beside the puppy on the kitchen floor, which is not ideal.

● Establish a daily routine. Most puppies sleep, then wake up and urinate, explore (maybe play) then urinate, eat then urinate (about 15 minutes after eating, although this varies with each individual), explore/rest (resist the temptation to play with your pup just after its meal – you could make it sick); defecate (about 30 minutes after eating – again this varies), sleep, then wake up and urinate, explore/play then urinate, and so on. There may be variations to this, but basically the process repeats itself ad nauseam. Read the section on toilet training (see pages 34–7).

● Leave your puppy alone when it is resting or sleeping. Never wake it up to play with it. You wouldn't disturb a sleeping baby, so why do it to a dog? If you overexcite or overtire your puppy, this will upset its routine and turn it into a grumpy, bad-tempered hooligan.

● Don't interact with your puppy every available waking moment. This will simply teach it to want to be the centre of attention and expect you to entertain it every time you appear – for the rest of its life. Plan regular 'quiet times' when your dog is to settle down and happily entertain itself with a toy.

● Everyone entering the puppy's area should ideally ignore it for at least 30 seconds (longer would be better) before they greet it. If you make a big fuss of the puppy the second you walk in, you will be creating an even bigger gulf between the richness of your company and the loneliness of its solitary confinement. You could be setting yourself up for separation problems later on, so make sure everyone who comes into contact with the puppy understands the importance of this advice – and complies with it.

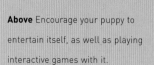

Above Encourage your puppy to entertain itself, as well as playing interactive games with it.

LIFTING OR CARRYING YOUR DOG

There are times when you will have to lift or carry your dog, such as when you take it to the vet's. It is therefore a good idea to practise this occasionally until the pair of you are familiar and comfortable with both the notion and the actuality. In this way, you will be able to avoid the indignity of having to cope with your dog trying to wriggle out of your arms and possibly becoming stressed, just when you need it to be calm and accepting.

Small dogs should be lifted and supported with one hand on their chest between their front legs, and the other between their back legs or around the backs of their thighs.

Big dogs can be scooped up with your arms around their bottom and chest.

Whether the dog is large or small, or somewhere in between, you should hold them upright and close to your body. Use flattened hands so that you don't grip or squeeze their skin.

Right This is a good way to carry a large dog, with your arms firmly around its shoulders and rear end.

THE FIRST EVENING AND NIGHT

You want your puppy to learn that it is not alone and that people will pop in regularly, but that this doesn't mean you will always come in response to noisy behaviour. Plan lots of rehearsals throughout the first day and evening so that your bundle of joy becomes used to the idea.

Below Puppies can be masters at manipulation, however, if it is used to being on its own for short periods, it won't panic at night.

If you are using a small crate as a bed, your puppy will need to be taken out frequently (even during the dead of night for the first few nights), as it should instinctively be unwilling to go to the toilet near its bed.

If you are using a larger crate or a small penned-off area, you can place the bedding at one end and the paper 'en-suite facilities' at the other. The dog is able to go to the toilet on the paper if it needs to, so it is less likely to wake you up in the middle of the night to be let out. However, it may, still wake you to come and clear up any mess, as dogs, like humans, do not like sharing their sleeping quarters with their waste products.

Try not to return to your puppy when it is whining, crying, barking or misbehaving in any other way. If you do, you are unwittingly rewarding undesirable behaviour, which might serve to make that behaviour worse in the long run. You should either wait until the behaviour has subsided or create a diversion to distract the puppy, THEN enter the room. Don't greet the puppy straight away – make a point of doing something else first (have a glass of water, for example), then go over to the puppy. This prevents problems later on with attention-seeking behaviour and overexcited greetings.

If it is necessary to let your puppy out or clean up after it, you should see to its needs without interacting with it. Don't look at it, speak to it or touch it – no matter how cute and adorable it is being – and absolutely no picking up and cuddling, otherwise your new pooch will learn that noisy behaviour or plaintive crying wins the 'jackpot', and it will only become progressively noisier over time.

THE NEXT MORNING

As soon as you are up and about the following morning, take the puppy outside to go to the toilet before you do anything else, even before putting the kettle or coffee pot on – no matter how dire your own need. As soon as your puppy wakes, it will need to urinate at the very least. When it has done so, put it back in its pen – now is the time to put the machine on for that much-needed shot of caffeine.

It is important to resist the desire to take the puppy out and play with it straight away; if you do, you will be setting yourself up for problems later (see the sections on attention-seeking behaviour, polite greeting behaviour and separation problems on pages 49–51, 52–3 and 54).

After a few days, when your puppy has a much better idea of where it should be going to the toilet, you can put the kettle on quickly before taking the dog out.

THE FIRST FEW DAYS

This may be the 'honeymoon period', but start as you mean to go on – no matter how appealing those soulful eyes may be. You'll make things more difficult if you don't.

Below Just as with children, it's very important to give your puppy the right start.

Allow the puppy at least 48 hours to settle in and get its bearings. Ideally, your puppy should sleep and spend most of its unsupervised time in a contained area, with frequent trips outside to go to the toilet.

Don't invite all your friends to visit too soon, as this can be overwhelming or even frightening. Let your puppy get used to its new family first. When introducing visitors, try to keep the puppy (and the guests) as calm as possible.

Everyone (especially children) must be made to understand that the puppy should be left alone when it is resting or sleeping. If you allow anyone to disturb its sleep pattern, you run the risk of making it overtired and grumpy.

Try to leave the puppy on its own for short periods every day (you can stay in the house, but the door between you should be closed), so that it doesn't become dependent on constant company. This should help prevent overattachment and separation problems later.

It is very dangerous to allow young puppies access to steps and stairs. Not only can they fall and seriously damage themselves, but also coming down stairs can strain and permanently damage their shoulders and elbows, causing lameness. Always carry them downstairs (and lift them out of cars or down other steep drops) unless they are too big to pick up, in which case only allow them to descend slowly with your hand in their collar. Once they are adults, this is less of a problem.

Never let your dog be a nuisance to anyone else. Be the guardian of polite dog manners. Don't let your dog jump up at you when you say 'hello' to it, or it will get into bad habits and think it is expected to jump up on everyone it meets. Make your dog sit when you and your guests say 'hello' to it. This can be difficult at first, but should become easier with practise. Owning a polite dog that has been taught to sit when people say 'hello' to it is a joy.

VET CHECK, VACCINATIONS AND WORMING

The sooner your puppy starts its course of vaccinations, the sooner it will be able to go out and about. This is very important if you want to socialize your dog properly (see pages 40–1).

Take your puppy to the veterinary clinic as soon as possible for a thorough check-up and also to start a regular worming and vaccination programme.

It is crucial that you regularly update your dog's vaccinations, as the major canine diseases can be fatal – and can act very quickly, too. Booster vaccinations are currently recommended at the same time every year. Your vet will be able to advise you appropriately.

Keep any vaccination certificates in a safe place, as you may need to show them should you ever want to kennel your dog, attend dog-training classes or take your dog to another country.

Your puppy also needs to be wormed regularly throughout its life. Purchase your dog's worming preparations from the veterinary surgery, and follow the vet's instructions regarding dosage.

Left The earlier your puppy begins vaccination, the earlier it can make its debut in the big, wide world.

TEACHING YOUR PUPPY ITS NAME

Only use your puppy's name in a positive way, using a toy or treat to condition it to come to you whenever you call it by name. Do not use your puppy's name as a correction, and never call it to you to chastise it, as you could set yourself up for horrendous problems later on when you want to call it back to you.

TOILET TRAINING

Young puppies have very poor bladder control – they need to be taken outside to relieve themselves very frequently. As a general guideline, they need to urinate immediately after waking from a nap and about 15 minutes after a meal, and they defecate about 30 minutes after eating. But they can also suddenly stop to urinate during a play session, so keep your eyes open for warning signs.

Don't expect your puppy to 'tell you' that it needs to go outside. It is far too young as yet to have learnt how to do that. However, most puppies will transmit at least some warning of their intentions by sniffing or circling. If they need to defecate, they often alter their tail carriage and start to arch their back. Squatting to urinate happens a lot more quickly, but it is more predictable. Nevertheless you have to be very quick to intercept them and take them to the right place.

If you do see any of the telltale signs, quickly but quietly scoop your puppy up and take it outside immediately. Stand still and be quiet or you will distract it. If it stops sniffing and sits down, move slowly away from the puppy until it gets up and follows, then stand still again (remaining quiet and avoiding all eye contact) until it urinates or defecates.

If your puppy is due to urinate or defecate in the garden, but won't 'go', it is highly likely that it will come back inside only to do it there. In this case, bring the puppy inside and keep it where you can watch it for the next ten minutes, then take it out again. Keep doing this until it performs – only then can you relax.

You should carry your puppy outside to the grass for the first few days, as the short walk to the back door may be too long or distracting to ensure success.

Even when it is able to make the journey successfully itself you should always go into the garden with the puppy when it is about to go to the toilet. The first reason for this is to attach a cue word (see below) to the appropriate action, one that is to be said only 'as and when' the pup successfully performs. You should also be out there to give a food treat to the puppy as a reward for going to the toilet correctly, This will help it to remember that going to the toilet outside is infinitely more profitable than doing it inside. A little well-chosen bribery goes a long way.

CUE WORDS

Teach your puppy to associate certain words or phrases, known as cue words, with relieving itself. Have different cue

Below Remember, any 'accidents' during toilet training are down to you and not the puppy.

words for urinating and defecating (I say 'Wee wees' and 'Poo poos'; others say 'Busy' and 'Quickly' – choose something you will feel comfortable using in public for years to come), and repeat these words every time the puppy goes to the toilet so that it begins to associate your chosen cue words with the appropriate action. Later on, you will be able to prompt your dog to go to the toilet on command by saying these words.

Use these toilet cues in an encouraging and praising tone while your puppy is actually performing, but try not to say 'Good boy' or 'Good girl', as it may take this to mean the evacuation command. You can guess what problems this may cause the next time you praise your dog!

AVOID TOILET-TRAINING ACCIDENTS

Every accident indoors is a nail in the coffin of toilet training so avoid them at all costs. The more urination and defecation that you can establish outside, the quicker the puppy's learning curve will be.

Only put newspaper on the floor at night and when your puppy is left on its own. Don't put the newspaper too close to the puppy's bed, as it won't want to spoil the area near its sleeping quarters. Put it where the puppy can easily find it and in the direction of the back door, so that you can gradually move the paper closer to the door over time. Remove the paper whenever you are there to supervise the puppy and take it outside, otherwise it will fall into the habit of going to the toilet indoors, and this can be a hard habit to break.

If you live in a flat or an apartment and do not have direct access to a garden or yard, you could (with your neighbour's permission) put a roll of grass turf on some plastic sheeting outside your front door (or on a safe balcony). This is a suitable stopgap measure until your pup learns the concept of going to the toilet outside, rather than indoors.

Never tell your puppy off when toilet training. The success, or otherwise, of the training is YOUR responsibility.

TOILET TRAINING TIPS

Toilet training should be quite a simple process. Sometimes owners tend to complicate matters by depending far too much on their puppy to understand their expectations, while neglecting their responsibility to spend time teaching the dog the appropriate behaviour. Mostly this can be put down to lack of routine or perhaps laziness on the owner's part.

You should set a proper feeding routine for your puppy, with meal times evenly spaced out over a 24-hour period, so that you can establish predictable toileting times. If you ensure regular input, you should receive regular output.

Feed the same type and amount of food at each meal as some foods pass through the digestive system faster than others, and this can upset the routine. Apart from the odd training treat, do not feed your puppy outside this routine or leave food down for it to eat as it pleases.

Do not overfeed your dog – take up any uneaten food within 15 minutes. Measure your dog's food (by weight or volume) at each meal. Most people overfeed their dogs routinely, and many dog food manufacturers are overly generous with recommended amounts. Do not feel bad if your dog is eating less than the suggested amount, but do cut down what you are offering so that it doesn't need to leave any.

Try to avoid bulky foods. Easily digestible and concentrated foods make toilet training less problematic because they produce the least amount of stools and urine. Your puppy should be passing a stool roughly 30 minutes after each meal.

Your puppy's stools should be consistently dark brown and firm. Overfeeding tends to produce large quantities of stools that are 'firm' at the beginning and 'soft' towards the end. Cut down the food slightly to see if this helps.

Loose, bulky or light-coloured stools can indicate a digestive problem or food intolerance, so it may be worth trying a change of food. However, if this continues consult your vet.

Keep a note of the times – a simple spreadsheet will work – when your puppy eats and actually goes to the toilet, as this will help you to determine its evacuation pattern and anticipate when it needs to go to the toilet. Obviously this will change as it grows older and its feeding regime changes, but a record will help you to keep up to date with the dog's latest patterns and so anticipate its needs.

Toilet training becomes easier with each success and deteriorates with each failure. The responsibility is yours to ensure that your puppy is never 'caught short' in the house.

Never punish the puppy if it has been to the toilet in the house. It is YOUR responsibility to ensure that it has a regular regime of opportunities to relieve itself outside, and this is only ever achieved with constructive toilet training.

Don't rub your dog's nose in its urine or faeces. This is cruel. No one would dream of rubbing a baby's face with a dirty nappy, so why they think it should work with dogs is difficult to imagine.

Right Feed your puppy at set times, as regular input produces regular output.

Likewise, shouting at your dog, making a noise with a rolled-up newspaper or calling your dog over to chastise it is really bad management. It will only confuse your dog and destroy its trust in you. Not only does this make the dog scared to come to you, but also it ruins your recall training (see page 58). Punished puppies often learn to go to the toilet in hidden places. Some dogs become really confused and even start eating the evidence.

Until your puppy is totally house-trained, don't give it unlimited access to the garden or backyard. As it grows older, it should learn to regulate itself to set frequent opportunities to go to the toilet (preferably associated with exercise, which will stimulate it to perform). Your puppy must learn to wait until these moments. In the meantime, take the puppy out regularly until you understand its needs better. An adult dog will usually urinate every three to four hours.

Only allow the puppy access beyond the the kitchen when you are convinced that it has nothing in its bladder or bowels; it cannot foul if there is nothing to expel. If you are at all in doubt, keep it either with you or where you can keep a close eye on it to anticipate any accidents, and take it out as soon as it shows signs of needing to go.

If your dog urinates because the greeting process overexcites it, don't greet it in the house. Take it into the garden or backyard before giving a much calmer greeting. Do not tell the dog off for this, or you will almost certainly make it worse.

Keep the garden or yard cleared of faeces or it won't go out there. Would you?

Never allow your dog to foul the footpath: train it to foul in the gutter by leading it there each time it tries to evacuate. Always take a plastic bag with you on your walks, so that you can clear up after any mess.

Don't take your dog's water away, as it will only drink to excess when you give the water back.

AVOIDING TEARS

It is not only the dog that needs training when you bring a puppy into your home. If you have children, they, too, need to be kept on a short(ish) leash when it comes to training and behaviour. It is important that they understand the following 'don'ts' when it comes to puppy love:

Don't put your face down next to the dog's, either for a hug or a cuddle. Many dogs really dislike close facial contact, unless they have initiated it themselves. Most dogs learn to be fairly tolerant, but occasionally they can snap (both metaphorically and physically). The resulting reaction can range from a warning snap, designed to deter you, to a full-blown temper tantrum and attack.

Don't ambush your dog or force yourself on it. If you want to fuss over it, invite the dog over, but do not force the issue if the dog doesn't want to go. It is important to leave the dog alone and give it space and peace when it wants it.

Don't torment your dog by blowing in its face, as this makes dogs progressively snappier towards faces. This is a common cause of facial bites.

Don't play rough and aggressive games with your puppy or dog, or it may become an expert at aggression later on.

Don't 'play fight' with each other or taunt the dog to make it protective or jealous. This can backfire badly if the dog ever misjudges the situation.

Don't allow or encourage the puppy to bite and hang onto your clothes, hands or feet, as this can be very hard to stop when the puppy gets bigger and stronger.

Over the page is a puppy poster designed to avoid common problems. Put a copy of this up where the puppy lives, so that you can refer the children – and the adults – to it whenever they break the rules.

HOUSE RULES

1 **Let sleeping dogs lie.** Leave your puppy alone when it is resting or sleeping. You're not allowed to wake a sleeping baby, so why do it to your puppy?

2 **Do not pick your puppy up or carry it around.** You could hurt it if you do. Call the puppy over to you if you want to make a fuss of it.

3 **Do not run around wildly or play rough games with the puppy, and do not let it bite you in play.** Only play gentle games with it or else you could hurt it or make it agitated.

4 **Never smack your puppy or shout at it.** This will make the puppy frightened and angry, and it might react by biting you.

5 **Teach your puppy to understand its commands.** It needs lessons every day. You can use treats to reward the puppy for sitting, lying down, coming when its name is called and walking with its lead on.

6 **Do not give your puppy the food that you are eating.** It should only eat dog food or its own special treats.

7 **Do not allow your puppy up on the beds or furniture.** If you want to stroke it, get down on the floor and call it over.

8 **Do not leave your toys or clothes on the floor where the puppy can steal them.** Put them away where it cannot reach them.

9 **Always give your puppy some fuss when it chooses to play with its own toys, and ignore it when it is being naughty.** Don't look at it, touch it or speak to it when it is misbehaving.

10 **Teach your friends to be very gentle with your puppy.** Stroke it quietly under its chin and along its back, and never pat it on the head. Do not kiss, cuddle or hug your puppy, as it may snap at your face or bite you.

ENJOY YOUR DOG – IT'S WONDERFUL

(Make sure you keep it that way!)

THE FIRST FEW MONTHS

The coming few months will be a period of intense learning for your puppy. At this age, it learns at a far faster rate than at any other time in its life. Although it may not yet be able to use what it learns, any knowledge gained will be stored for future use. Do not be fooled into thinking that your puppy is just a baby with a childish mentality. Although it may just be a puppy, its brain is fully developed, and it will crave knowledge with which to fill it. This is why they are so curious.

What your puppy learns (or is allowed to learn) during this period will ultimately shape its character. It will also determine your puppy's relationship with you and its attitude to its environment.

It is important that you understand that your puppy will learn from every experience now, regardless of whether that was your intention or not. Your responsibility is to make sure that it learns useful and positive lessons that will benefit it and prepare it for adult life. You should also try to anticipate and control any negative experiences and try to ensure that it does not learn or pick up any bad habits that could cause behavioural problems later.

You simply cannot afford to waste this formative period. If you let things run their natural course without any forethought or planning, you run the risk of your puppy developing bad habits and associations that will haunt you when it is an adult. As with everything in life, an ounce of prevention is worth a pound of cure.

INTRODUCING THE COLLAR AND LEAD

After a day or two, your puppy should be settled enough to be introduced to a lightweight nylon puppy collar. Put it on for short periods at feeding time or when playing in the garden or yard. You can expect your puppy to scratch a lot at first, and it may even throw a tantrum. It is best to ignore this behaviour, or try to distract it with titbits or a game to take its mind off it. Until the puppy is used to the collar, don't leave it on when it is unsupervised, as it could get a foot caught in it.

As the puppy grows, you should check the size of the collar to ensure it is not too tight. The collar should be loose enough to get two fingers easily inside it but tight enough to prevent it from being pulled off over the puppy's head.

After a few days of using the collar, begin 'lead training'. Attach a light piece of string or cord 1 metre (3 feet) long and let the puppy drag it around. Don't use the real lead, and don't worry if the puppy chews it – you can always tie it together

Above Collar and lead training should be started very early on.

again, as it is only a piece of string. The important thing is that the puppy must NOT learn to associate the lead with a barrage of correction and nagging.

When the puppy will happily drag around the piece of string, you can pick up the string and lure it to follow you for some treats (or a toy) in your hand. The idea is to go slowly enough to capture and maintain the puppy's interest. Hold your arm out to the side, and offer the reward where you would like its nose to finish up.

Chat to the puppy to keep its attention for a few steps, then stop and give the reward at the side of your leg, so that the puppy is rewarded for being in the right position.

Only reward sensible walking. If the puppy is overkeen and jumps up or snatches at its treat, accelerate slightly until it has to walk normally (which it will have to do if it wants to keep up), then reward it. If the dog is uninterested in keeping up, slow down and be more obvious with the lure. You may need to find a better lure, reward more frequently or work with fewer distractions.

If the puppy panics and freezes on the spot and will not be coaxed forwards, do not force the issue or drag it around. Just drop the string and walk away, leaving it to realize that nothing bad will happen, other than losing out on the attention and rewards. It should recover quite quickly, and you can resume training later on.

Once the puppy is following you reliably, pick up the string, keeping it completely loose while you are walking. When you stop to reward the puppy, apply (and release) a tiny bit of pressure from the lead, just before you dispense your reward. This is to teach the puppy not to panic when it feels pressure on its neck.

Once the puppy is used to this, you can introduce your normal walking lead.

It is essential that the puppy is used to wearing a collar and lead at home and in the garden before taking it out 'for real', otherwise the novelty and discomfort can distract and inhibit the pup. It may even make its first trip outdoors traumatic.

Don't forget to order an engraved identity disc with your name and address on it for your dog's collar. Refer to page 117 for more information.

ENVIRONMENTAL FAMILIARIZATION

Use this formative period to teach your puppy pleasant associations with things and situations that may frighten it later in life, such as traffic, crowds of people, vets, car travel, traffic noise and movement, adult dogs and children.

Lack of early socialization is a common cause of serious problems later, so take your puppy out every day for short

Left Ensure your puppy always wears its collar and engraved identity disc when outside.

'educational' trips in the car, to the local shops, and so on. Until it has completed its vaccination course, your puppy should not be put down on the ground outside, so carry it around these places in your arms or allow it to gain a window on the world from the safety of the car.

Make each new association a positive experience by using food treats and liberal praise, but don't put your puppy into any frightening situations where it may feel insecure or worried. Groups of schoolchildren or heavy traffic can be overwhelming to a shy or timid puppy.

If your puppy is a little frightened or apprehensive, do NOT stroke it or praise it. Instead of comforting it, you are actually rewarding its fearful behaviour and teaching it to be timid. If you can, give the puppy time to work things out for itself with as little interference from you as possible, or 'jolly' it through the experience, showing it by your reaction that there is nothing to be worried about. At the first sign of success, remove the puppy from the situation, then try again a little later on. If it does not improve with time, you should seek specialist help.

SOCIALIZING WITH OTHER DOGS

Once they have been fully vaccinated, most dogs need regular 'off lead' exercise to satisfy their mental and physical needs. They need to play with their own species on a daily basis. It is not enough only to walk dogs at the weekends, as they tend to redirect their energies into undesirable behaviour. All too often, bad behaviour is caused by frustration of natural instincts.

It is hugely important that your puppy is given sufficient opportunity to learn how to interact with adult dogs so that it grows up without any hang-ups or inhibitions. Introduce your puppy to some temperamentally sound adult dogs as soon as its vaccination programme is finished (or earlier if it is meeting a vaccinated dog in a private garden). A safe adult dog (or bitch) is one that is more than two years old, but not in double figures; mixes 'off lead' with other dogs every day; and is tolerant of puppies, but will curb them fairly (but not excessively) if they deserve it. Most owners know what their dogs are like, so ask your dog-owning friends if they can help you.

If your puppy is annoying the adult dog, it should be allowed to 'tick it off' for impolite behaviour. As long as the discipline is deserved, don't interfere. Most adult dogs are incredibly tolerant of puppies up to a point, after which they have to put the puppy in its place. This will teach it its canine 'Ps and Qs', and it is a very important lesson for it to learn while it is still protected by 'puppy status'.

Until your puppy starts showing some respect to other dogs, try not to let it mix too regularly with other puppies or young dogs (under two years old), as they will most probably overstimulate each other into wild, uninhibited behaviour.

For the same reason, do not let your puppy run around with other young puppies or juveniles at puppy parties, playgroups or dog-training classes. They will often make each other wild, rather than teaching each other manners. You wouldn't expect a group of three-year-old children to teach each other manners when left to their own devices, and the same is true of puppies.

Most puppies will back down from an adult dog, but not from another puppy. If it hasn't learnt its canine manners before it reaches puberty, it may run into problems later on. Most dogs are less inclined to correct another adult because they don't want to risk being answered back or starting a fight. Ensure your puppy learns to respect adult dogs before it is too late.

Below Meeting adult dogs will teach your puppy manners and help to ensure that is is properly socialized.

3 TEACHING GOOD MANNERS

There are times when raising and training a puppy can seem remarkably like launching into the joys, trials and tribulations of raising a child – a sort of canine version of toddler taming. While treating your dog like a human is not a good idea, there are parallels to be drawn between the two. Curiosity, a knack for getting into what they shouldn't, exploring their boundaries and attention-seeking behaviour are all part of the learning process. Most of the problems you may encounter are common ones and entirely predictable. Getting it right need not be as overwhelming as it might seem, as long as you adopt the right approach.

THE BEST APPROACH

START ALL NEW TRAINING IN A QUIET PLACE

Begin your training somewhere familiar with the least number of distractions, such as your home or garden. There is no point taking a puppy outside and expecting it to ignore all the distractions and focus entirely on you. That's a bit like taking a child to Disneyland for the first time and expecting it to learn logarithms.

Once your dog thoroughly understands a lesson at one level, gradually increase the distractions until the conditions simulate reality. You can then extend your training to different environments. This helps your dog to be reliable under a variety of conditions and increases your chances of success.

KEEP ALL TRAINING SESSIONS SIMPLE AND SHORT

Puppies have a really short attention span, so it is important not to make the session too long or to nag and confuse them. The golden rules of successful dog training are: 'Quit while you're ahead' and 'Leave them wanting more'. Don't confuse your puppy by teaching it several things during the same session. Pick one exercise, practise it a couple of times and reward your puppy richly – then allow it to relax to reflect on and absorb that lesson.

GET YOUR TIMING RIGHT

Commands given too early – and praise given too late – can be a major source of confusion to a learning dog. Ensure that your commands are associated with the dog's compliant behaviour. Keep repeating the command along with the praise, for example, 'Good sit!' Praise, command and reward should be simultaneous, so that your puppy is in absolutely no doubt as to what it is being praised for and exactly which command goes with it.

ALWAYS HAVE AN 'OFF SWITCH'

Using a release command or phrase (such as 'that will do' or 'off you go') after each successful action is vital. This acts as an 'off switch' and tells your puppy when it can rise, thus ending the exercise consistently. Try not to use 'OK' or 'come on' as release commands, as these are often used in everyday conversation and could lead to all kinds of confusion.

USE REALLY TASTY TREATS

Food can be a very effective tool in training a young puppy. Real food treats (such as liver tablets, shavings of dried tripe stick, or food scraps) tend to work better than shop-bought processed 'treats'. See page 102 for ideas. Just make sure that you don't drop the treats on the floor and allow your dog to find them – this will only teach it to scavenge.

DEVELOP A WIDER RANGE OF INTERESTING REWARDS

Don't rely exclusively on food to reward your puppy. As it grows, it will probably lose interest in food as a primary reward and become much more interested in being fussed over or playing games involving toys. Cultivate 'toy games' with your puppy so that you have a common interest later on. It may become necessary to condition the dog into a particular type of toy or treat that is used only for training purposes. Doing this can increase the dog's perceived value of the reward. Rewards that are too easily available can lose their attraction, whereas a rationed toy or treat should retain its appeal.

TRAIN THE FAMILY (AND FRIENDS) TO BE CONSISTENT

Draw up a list of commands, signals and training techniques, and ensure that everyone in the household uses them consistently. Any variation will only confuse the puppy and retard its learning. How can you expect to stop a young puppy from chasing and play-biting the children if the children are calling and encouraging it to chase them at the same time?

BE PATIENT

Dogs may be intelligent, but, like humans, they learn at different speeds. Continue training and reinforcing good behaviour until it becomes built-in or 'default'.

Anything less than this ingrained response could break under strain at a later date.

NEVER PUNISH OR BECOME ANGRY WITH YOUR DOG

Losing your temper only teaches your dog to believe that you are capable of abuse and aggressive behaviour of your own. At best, this confuses your dog; at worst, you

can permanently destroy its trust in you. All corrections should be humane and constructive, and followed by a deeply convincing demonstration of the benefits of exhibiting the correct behaviour.

Below Be patient and constructive. Never lose your temper with your dog – it will be counterproductive.

WHY SAYING 'NO' SO OFTEN FAILS

If saying 'no' were the great training solution, I would recommend it. The truth is that it fails more often than it succeeds for a variety of reasons:

● When you make a fuss, you are simply drawing attention to the 'forbidden fruit', which of course makes it even more attractive – dogs can be all too human in this regard.

● If your dog realizes that you are the designated punishment dispenser, it will simply wait until you have gone out before it misbehaves.

● Punishment often comes too late for the dog to learn to associate it with the unwanted action.

● Some dogs just don't care if you are angry. For them, the benefits of the behaviour outweigh your correction.

● Dogs eventually become accustomed to nagging and learn to ignore it – sound familiar?

● If the dog is frustrated because it doesn't have a suitable outlet for its energy, it needs to be taught an appropriate alternative behaviour.

● Saying 'no' teaches the dog how to obtain your immediate attention. This is why so many dogs appear to be 'professionally naughty'.

PAWS FOR THOUGHT

● Never call your dog to you for a punishment, and never punish it after it has finished being naughty. Correction should coincide with the undesirable action. Calling it to the scene of the 'crime' to chastise it will only teach your dog not to come when called.

● Never use a rolled-up newspaper to punish your puppy, and do not smack your puppy or shout at it. This type of aggression only makes it nervous and suspicious of hands and faces. Using force or fear to bully a dog will eventually fail when the dog becomes big enough and bold enough to answer back or get in first – and you certainly never want to enter into an 'arms race' with your dog.

● Don't put your dog away on its own in the kitchen or outside as a punishment. Instead, teach it to settle (see page 79) or tolerate being tethered. If it becomes too boisterous, temporarily tether it (with a chew toy) in the corner of the room until it calms down, then let it free. Doing this teaches the dog that bad behaviour means restraint, while good behaviour gets it off the hook (literally).

Right Be positive. Encourage your dog to exhibit good manners with positive reinforcement, not threats.

SO HOW SHOULD YOU CORRECT A DOG?

🐾 You need to make it easy for the 'preferred' behaviour to happen. Teach and make the preferred behaviour irresistible or hugely rewarding for the dog. For example, you could teach it to 'settle' (see page 79).

🐾 Pretend to ignore your puppy when it is being naughty. Don't look at, touch or speak to it, particularly if the behaviour was designed to attract your attention in the first place. When the puppy stops the undesirable behaviour, you can divert it into the preferred option, then reward it handsomely with your attention.

🐾 If the behaviour is impossible to ignore because it is dangerous, potentially expensive or irritating, create a diversion or consequence (see pages 48–9) at the exact scene of the 'crime'. You need to interrupt the behaviour and distract (and possibly deter) the dog long enough to create a window of opportunity to give it a greater reward for stopping. The dog can then be cued into a preferred behaviour.

🐾 Ensure that the diversion and its consequence is a distraction, rather than a reward (such as food, a toy or a game). You don't want to unwittingly reward the 'wrong' behaviour. Also, it is vital that the dog does not discover that the diversion or consequence came from you.

🐾 Don't laugh or stare at the dog while the diversion or consequence takes place, or immediately afterwards, otherwise it will link you to the correction – defeating the purpose of the entire exercise.

Below Be on your best behaviour: don't share your food at the table, as it only encourages begging.

SQUELCHING THOSE BAD HABITS

Wherever possible, try to make the correction for 'bad' behaviour appear to come from whatever your puppy was interfering with. It is also important to remember that any correction should come while – and never after – the 'crime' is being committed. In this way your dog learns a negative association with the action and not with YOU.

With a little planning, it is quite easy to 'set up' your puppy so that it learns from its experiences. You want it to learn that some of its activities are risky, possibly even dangerous. This will give it a much better reason to avoid repeating that error.

THE DIVERSION METHOD

A fine jet of water is subtly delivered from a concealed 'squirter'. Those little plastic lemon-juice dispensers seem to work best, but rinse them thoroughly first. You can use a water pistol but only do so if you can easily conceal it in your hand. Don't use a plant-spray bottle, as it is too visible.

Be subtle about the squirting. Don't point, aim and squirt, as your puppy will see you in its peripheral vision, giving the game away. Hold the squirter close to your body, and do not obviously look at the dog or laugh when he reacts.

You can squirt the dog anywhere on the body, but the most effective targets – if your aim is up to it – are rear ends and faces. Your puppy will feel something land on its body, but won't know that it's only water. It should be startled, successfully diverting or deterring it from whatever it was doing. Remember, secrecy is key, so use this method prudently. Don't overuse it, and never let your children play with the squirter – the effect will be lost forever because they lack the necessary stealth to carry out this type of covert operation.

NOISE DETERRENTS

If your puppy is undeterred by the 'secret squirt', and as long as it is not nervous or sound-sensitive, you can try using noise

Left The diversion method can help you in your goal to prevent your dog taking over the furniture.

deterrents to startle it out of stealing and raiding garbage cans, laundry baskets, kitchen tables and dishwashers. This is a great lesson in consequences.

Try gently lobbing an empty drink can with some pebbles inside (a 'rattle can') or a couple of lightweight cake or biscuit tin lids, so that they land next to the puppy at the exact moment that it is committing the crime – only attempt this diversion if your aim is good. The dog will momentarily startle, and you should immediately remove the noise deterrent from sight, then praise your puppy for stopping the undesired behaviour.

The puppy must never know that the correction came from you, so do not show your 'weapon of choice' before throwing it or threaten the dog with it. This will demystify the 'magic' of the correction, and inevitably your puppy will still carry out its crimes – only it will employ some stealth of its own and wait until you're not around to correct it. The aim is to give your puppy a nasty shock that is associated purely with the crime it was committing.

If your dog repeatedly steals when your back is turned, set up a concealed or disguised (covered with a sheet of newspaper) 'booby trap' made up of light cake tin lids or 'rattle cans', and balance them precariously on a shelf above the

'lure'. Tie a piece of cotton thread to the lids or cans, and attach the other end below the booby trap to the article your puppy is likely to steal. When the puppy investigates, it will receive a shock when it disturbs the article and the concealed 'alarm' comes crashing down near it.

Repeat this in different places, until the offending article remains undisturbed – your inquisitive pup will have learnt its lesson. Don't let it watch you set up the booby trap, and do make sure that you wait around to reappear the minute the puppy sets it off, so that you can remove the trap before the dog investigates.

This method will not work if food is the bait, as the reward will probably outweigh the correction. Always put food away or out of your dog's reach – much like children, dogs cannot resist putting their paws into the proverbial cookie jar.

LONG LINE
A long line – a 2 metre (6 feet) length of string – can also be used for control while you are at home with your puppy. (Always remove the line when your puppy is unsupervised so that it cannot get itself caught up in anything.) This helps you to stop the dog in its tracks and regain possession of anything it has stolen, preventing it from manipulating you

into a frustrating and ultimately unrewarding game of chase.

ATTENTION-SEEKING BEHAVIOUR
Does crime pay in your house, or do you have a professional goody-goody? Puppies invariably learn that certain activities are practically guaranteed to gain your attention, as many households unwittingly reward their dog by giving it more attention for being 'naughty' than they do for being good.

Some of the more annoying actions, such as stealing, not only demand the owner's immediate attention, but also instigate a guaranteed game of chase. Most owners find it impossible to ignore this kind of behaviour. Although they may chastise the dog, the dog still wins through manipulation and forcing its owners to interact with it.

This is the reason why so many dogs are 'professionally naughty' – not because they are bad, but because they are clever and have learnt that one behaviour is more successful or interesting than another. Never reward this behaviour with your attention, as you will merely perpetuate it. So, how can you call a halt to this cycle of attention seeking without being suckered in?

STEALING PERSONAL ITEMS

Puppies commonly steal strongly scented items such as socks, shoes, spectacles, hair accessories, pens, wallets, remote controls, clothes, children's favourite toys – the list goes on and on. If you see your puppy with one of these in its mouth, either ignore it or use a diversion and consequence, or long line (see page 62).

Ensure that the puppy has much more interesting (and safe) chew toys, and make an extra big fuss of it when it decides to play with them instead. Try to keep harmful items out of the dog's reach, and teach children to clear up anything they would not want to lose to the dog.

CHEWING

Most puppies explore in much the same way that small babies do: they put things into their mouths. In most cases, it is rejected after a little chew, as they lose interest and move on. Where this goes wrong is when owners ignore the puppy when it chews the right things, but react very obviously and instantly when the dog chews the wrong things. Your little darling will quickly learn what works best to elicit your instant and undivided attention.

If you see your puppy chewing something it shouldn't, administer a secret squirt or throw something noisy such as a rattle can or keys to interrupt the behaviour, then simply divert and encourage it onto something more suitable.

If your puppy is chewing furniture when you aren't there, smear a little clove oil (available from a chemist or pharmacy) onto greaseproof paper, then cover the chewed area with this for a few days. The clove oil acts as a taste deterrent, so be careful not to get the smell on your hands.

MOUTHING (PLAYBITING)

Experimental biting is a natural play behaviour between puppies. They do not grow out of this, so you will have to teach your puppy that it is not allowed to use its teeth on your flesh or clothing, under any circumstances.

Mouthing is most likely to happen at moments of great excitement or irritation, so it is important to have appropriate toys to hand when playing or greeting. This is

Left Encourage your dog to chew or mouth its toys – appropriate ones, of course – and not you.

especially necessary for gun dogs, which were selectively bred to pick up and carry when excited. If the puppy mouths you accidentally when you are playing with it, pick up a toy and divert the mouthing onto the toy. Shake the toy gently, and praise the puppy when it bites the toy.

Do not incite or encourage your dog to playbite clothing or flesh. Hugging and kissing dogs frequently irritates them into snapping at faces, while running children tend to incite ankle chasing. Owners who wrestle their dogs only encourage play fighting and biting, and these dogs can become progressively rougher and more difficult for their owners to handle over time.

Persistent or deliberate mouthing should be interrupted with a secret squirt of water or a noise deterrent. The puppy should then be ignored for a few minutes to communicate your disdain.

Lots of dogs dislike it when hands are passed over their heads, and this incites them into mouthing the offending hand. Instead of trying to pat or stroke your puppy on the top of its head, show it your open hand, with the palm uppermost, then stroke it under the jaw – this is a less offensive initial approach. Puppies love having their jaw, neck and chest rubbed, as well as having their backs rubbed just above their tails.

Children and people who are apprehensive of dogs often try to pat them on their heads. This can unnerve a dog. Direct them away from touching the top of its head or pulling their hands away suddenly, in case they frighten the dog. Show them the correct way to stroke it under the chin (or along the back if they don't want to go near the mouth). Encourage them to follow your hand movements, giving both the dog and the person confidence.

PAWING

Dogs that are taught early in their life to use their paws to perform a trick – such as giving a paw or a high-five – will commonly progress to seeking attention by scratching their nails down their owners' legs and arms. This can be painful, but can be avoided if you don't teach your dog to give a paw until it is about a year old. Dogs that are taught other tricks first and only later in their training how to use their paws do this significantly less.

If your dog is scratching you to seek your attention, teach it to lie down and settle on its bed (see page 79). Use this technique every time the dog tries to scratch you – it should soon lose the habit.

Left Wait until your dog is old enough before teaching it to give a paw.

BARKING

Barking for attention can be extremely difficult to ignore, so it often gets your dog what it wants. Whatever you do, don't shout at your dog when it is being vocal – it might think you're joining in.

Try distracting your puppy with a secret squirt of water (see page 46), then give it attention for being quiet. As long as everyone stops responding to the barking, your puppy should soon lose interest and give it up as a bad job.

Make sure that you do not unwittingly encourage your dog to be excessively vocal by teaching it to bark by the back door. It may not be able to distinguish the difference between that behaviour and barking just for attention.

MOUNTING

Mounting can sometimes seem like the ultimate social embarrassment for a dog owner. There they are trying to impress their new boss, love interest or mother-in-law, and their dog commits the seemingly unforgivable faux pas of mounting. In fact, mounting is not necessarily sexually motivated, and you should feel neither flattered nor embarrassed, regardless of whether or not you are the one on the receiving end. Many puppies mount objects or each other either to instigate play or to 'dominate'. If your puppy starts mounting excessively around the same age that he starts to cock his leg, it's because he is going through adolescence. If your pup mounts you, get up and walk away, deter it with a secret squirt of water or distract it with a noise deterrent. If the behaviour worsens, or the dog is an adult, seek advice from your vet.

'MUGGING' VISITORS FOR ATTENTION

If your puppy is being demanding when you have visitors, ignore it. If it is really uncontrollable, teach it the settle (see page 79) or try tethering it to something very secure, with a chew toy to occupy it, and only untether it once it has calmed down.

Ask visitors not to make eye contact with your puppy, but instead simply to ignore it. It may try anything to gain their attention, but insist that they do not make eye contact until it is much more relaxed. When your puppy is calm, release it – but keep it on a long line so that you can regain control easily if it starts to demand attention again.

This is better than shutting your puppy alone in another room, as being isolated only frustrates it more and leads to even worse behaviour when it is brought back in. Keeping your puppy under control in the same room as you is like putting a child into a playpen – they are still included, but are prevented from being the centre of attention. It allows them to learn that settling down is the key to being released.

POLITE GREETING BEHAVIOUR

Unless taught otherwise, most puppies and young dogs believe that jumping up is the expected 'greeting protocol'. They have usually been unwittingly trained by their owners to become overexcited and jump up whenever they hear the word 'hello'. Whether you welcome the jumping up or try to correct it, the dog expects and receives your immediate attention, so this routine becomes established as the 'default greeting behaviour'.

Don't let your dog jump up at you when you say 'hello' to it, or it might think it is OK to jump up at other people. Dogs that are allowed to jump up on their owners and visitors think nothing of jumping up on complete strangers in the street or children in the park. This can get you and your dog into serious trouble. Never let your dog be a nuisance to anyone else. Teach it polite manners.

Be consistent. Training won't work if only some of the family members are trying to train the dog, while others are unwittingly or constructively confusing it.

Make your dog sit when you and your guests say 'hello' to it. This might be difficult at first, but should become easier with practise. Each time it jumps up, hold its collar and place it in the 'sit' position (see pages 66–7). You may have to hold the dog there while you fuss over it, until it learns that polite sitting is the key to receiving a warm welcome. Do this until it becomes automatic.

If this does not bring about sufficient improvement, try turning and walking away the moment your dog jumps up on you. When its front feet have hit the floor again, immediately turn around, place the dog in the sit position and make a fuss of it again. This teaches the dog that jumping 'switches people off' and that the more polite approach (sitting) will ensure that it gets what it wants.

Alternatively, routinely ignore your dog for a count of 30 seconds (maybe put the kettle on or read a few lines of the newspaper) every time you or anyone else walks into the house. Then call the dog onto its bed, and ask it to sit for a quality fuss. Give it some treats there, too, as this helps to speed the learning process. Keep the treat pot near your dog's bed.

If everybody is consistent, your dog will soon be patiently sitting on its bed, mentally counting down and staring at its treat pot in expectation every time someone comes in.

If the jumping up is impossible to ignore, put the lead on and tread on it to keep the dog at floor level. Don't let go of the other end of the lead in case the dog pulls free from you. Ignore the dog (don't look at it, touch it or speak to it) until it tires and stops for a breather, then praise it enthusiastically for NOT jumping up. Be prepared to withdraw your fussing as soon as your dog starts jumping again, and resume the praise as soon as it stops.

Most puppies will try to jump up and greet everyone they meet when they first start going out. The best way to work through this is to walk your puppy around (on a lead) regularly where there are lots of people. The novelty will eventually wear off and it will realize that not all people were put on this earth to greet it.

If people do stop to talk to your dog, place it in the sit position or tread on the lead (but keep hold of the other end) to prevent it from jumping up, and do not let anyone encourage the dog to jump up.

Above Teach your dog to curb its unbridled enthusiasm and instead greet people politely and calmly.

AVOIDING SEPARATION ANXIETY

It is important that you do not allow (or encourage) your dog to be clingy and overdependent on your constant company. If you do, you will not be able to leave it on its own, even for short periods, without the risk of it becoming stressed.

Unless they are properly prepared for being left alone, dogs can suffer from 'separation anxiety'. Unfortunately, they tend to express their stress and frustration by crying, howling, barking, chewing, digging, scratching, stealing, mutilating themselves or fouling, so you'll want to prevent this for your own sake, as well as the dog's. Preventive training is best:

Allow your puppy to become used to being separated from you while you are still in the house. Don't let it sleep in any of the bedrooms or curl up on your lap or lie on your feet. Dogs that sleep with their owners are far more likely to develop separation stress than those accustomed to sleeping on their own.

Keep your internal doors shut until your puppy learns to accept it as 'normal', and not something that is open to negotiation. Alternatively, use child gates to control its access.

Let your puppy become accustomed to being left alone in the room that it sleeps in, as a matter of course, for brief periods several times a day. While the dog is there, it will become used to the sound of activity elsewhere, including doors opening and closing, while you remain in the house for the sake of safety.

Right Take time to ensure that your dog is used to being left on its own.

TITBITS

● Don't make a drama of going out. Allow a cooling-off and settling-down period where your dog is confined to its room for 10 minutes before you go out, during which time it receives no attention from you. Doing this prevents it from becoming overstimulated before you go on your way.

● Frequently leave the dog for short periods, so that it accepts this as part of everyday life. Tire your dog out with a good walk or a game first, so that it is both physically and mentally tired and has recently been to the toilet. Make sure that it has water and plenty of chew toys to occupy it, and leave the radio on in an adjoining room (talk radio is ideal) so it doesn't know whether you are in or not.

● On your return, don't go straight to your dog. Spend a few minutes doing other things before letting it out. This stops it thinking that receiving immediate attention is its divine right and also teaches it not to become impatient or demanding.

● Always let it out into the garden for to urinate first, and delay saying 'hello' for about 30 seconds, so it does not mug you the second you walk in the door. Greet it in its bed area, while making it sit, so you reinforce polite greeting manners.

PAWS FOR THOUGHT

Never use confinement as a punishment. Many owners shut their dogs in another room, or in the garden or backyard, when they are naughty or seeking attention. This only serves to frustrate the dog even more, and it is likely to develop problems. Teach the settle (see page 79), so this is unnecessary.

Don't punish your dog for any damage or chastise it on your return. This merely increases its stress levels, which may make it progressively worse. If you are experiencing separation problems, ask your vet to recommend someone to help your dog overcome them.

4 BASIC TRAINING

It really doesn't take a great deal of effort to train your dog in the basic exercises, especially if you tackle things in the right way. A little time devoted to this early on can spare you and your dog from more complicated difficulties further down the track. Training can and should be fun for both of you, so keep it short and sweet. This way, neither you nor the dog will become bored. Use rewards liberally to encourage your dog to learn faster – it always helps to sweeten the pill. You simply have to take the time, and you will end up with an exemplary pooch that is more 'Best in Show' than painful prima donna.

HERE, BOY!

Recall is simply when you call your dog to come back to you. A good recall is one of the most important things that you will ever teach your dog. It is essential in an emergency, when you may need the dog to come to you immediately. Quite apart from this, it is really not fair to keep your dog on a lead if you go to a park where other dogs are allowed off their leads. It's rather like taking a child to a funfair, but not letting them take any of the rides. Being constantly on the leash can cause many problems, including huge amounts of frustration and bad behaviour on the part of both the dog and the owner. If you teach your dog a reliable recall early on, you can confidently and safely let your dog have free-running exercise in a safe area.

Many novice owners are too scared to allow their young puppy to run free off the lead until they have perfected the recall, but this can delay and adversely affect their puppy's social development and recall training. You can often get round this problem by exercising the dog on a trailing long line (see page 62).

Fortunately, young puppies (less than four months old) are quite insecure and clingy, and they tend not to stray very far from their owners, even when there are other dogs around. This makes it the best time to introduce them to the local park, where they can meet and socialize with a wide range of dogs and learn their canine 'Ps and Qs', with little danger of them running off.

If you don't let your puppy off lead until it is older, say about four to five months old, it will be a little more independent, far more easily distracted and slightly more difficult to control and train.

If you wait until it is six months or older before you let it meet other dogs off the lead, you may miss the critical socialization period entirely – although you should always try socializing your dog. You will also have produced a dog that cannot wait to get away from you and becomes wildly overexcited and frustrated at the sight of other dogs. In short, you will have your very own canine hooligan, and all because it never had the chance to learn more appropriate behaviour.

It is therefore important that you make it a priority to teach your puppy to come to you by calling it and rewarding it when it approaches you, whether it be for a game, toy, treats or dinner. You should also give your dog more formal training, as described here.

BASIC RECALL TRAINING

1 SET ASIDE A FEW MINUTES FOR EACH TRAINING SESSION. Offer an enticing reward, such as a favourite toy or some tasty treats. This type of recall is between you and the puppy – in other words, you are calling it on your own. Choose a time and a place with no other distractions – in the house, garden or backyard are ideal.

2 BEGIN WITH THE DOG ON THE LEAD. Wait until the puppy's attention has wandered, then

Below Wait until your dog is looking away before calling it.

Left Call cheerfully, flick the lead and show the reward while running backwards, praising the dog all the way as it comes in to you.

call its name enthusiastically; give a little flick on the lead (enough to make it turn and look at you). Show it the reward right in front of its nose, then run backwards, 'luring' it to follow and catch up with you.

3 SHOWER PRAISE ON YOUR PUPPY. Keep this up the entire time it is coming towards you. Slow down and let it catch up with you after about 10 metres (30 feet). Crouch down to the dog's level, and coax it all the way in to you. Dispense the reward from one hand, and take hold of the puppy's collar with your other. Reach for the collar from under the dog's chin, not over — many dogs will back away from you if you pass a hand over their heads. Give the dog the reward, but make a big fuss of

Below Crouch down, take hold of the dog's collar and fuss over and reward the dog.

it as well, as you do not want to become too reliant on the treat. Play vigorously with the toy, if that's what your dog prefers.

4 REPEAT THIS A COUPLE OF TIMES IN EACH TRAINING SESSION. This way, the dog will retain the idea, but not become bored. Have several small sessions throughout the day.

5 INCREASE THE VARIETY OF PLACES WHERE YOU TRAIN. Good practical places would be right outside your house, in case your dog ever gets out; walking down the street, in case its collar were to break; in a friend's garden and in a variety of parks.

6 PROGRESS TO DISTRACTION TRAINING (see page 60). Your puppy must first come to you reliably in a range of circumstances. Then you can test it over greater distances using a trailing long line (see page 62).

DISTRACTION TRAINING

Once the puppy has learnt the basic recall concept, it needs to learn to come away from interesting distractions when you call to it – and you need another person to help you do this. Calling between two of you is vital to distraction training.

1 SELECT A FAMILIAR, NON-DISTRACTING ENVIRONMENT, SUCH AS YOUR HOUSE OR GARDEN. Walk near enough to the dog to gain its attention. Next call the dog and offer the reward by showing the chosen toy or treat – just moving slowly will catch its eye. Run backwards, encouraging the dog to follow you, praising it all the way. When it catches up with you, crouch down and coax it all the way in to you. Always touch the collar with your other hand, before handing over the reward.

2 GIVE THE REWARD TO THE DOG, AND MAKE A BIG FUSS OF IT. After a minute of lavish attention, stand up and studiously ignore the pup (no looking, touching or talking), so that it starts to lose interest in you. When this happens, the other person should come forwards and call the dog, offer the reward and run backwards, encouraging the dog to follow them, and so on.

3 NOW ALTERNATE CALLING THE DOG BETWEEN THE TWO OF YOU. Only practise a maximum of two recalls for each person in each session. Don't go on and on, as it can be counterproductive. Remember the golden rules of dog training: 'Always quit while you're ahead' and 'Leave the dog wanting more.'

Left Call, run backwards, crouch down and hold the collar while praising and rewarding the dog.

Left Stand up and ignore the dog while the second person calls.

4 KEEP PRACTISING DISTRACTION TRAINING OVER A PERIOD OF A FEW DAYS. The dog will learn to predict the familiar routine of running backwards and forwards between two people. Reward the dog's initiative in order to raise its confidence levels. Your dog is also learning to leave an existing distraction (in other words, the nearest person with unavailable rewards) for the promise – and delivery – of a more distant but guaranteed reward (at the hands of the second person).

5 NOW TAKE THE TRAINING ON A STAGE FURTHER. The first person calls and rewards the dog as usual. The dog will expect the second person to call it next and so run to them. At this stage, you play 'contrary': the second person does not call and studiously ignores the dog (no eye contact, no speaking, no touching) until it loses interest in them. The first person then calls the dog to them and rewards it when it gets there. The dog will then probably hang around the first person (having lost interest in the second).

If this happens, the first person should ignore it, while the second person calls and rewards. The dog will learn that every time it tries to predict where to go next, it is wrong. Soon it will give up guessing and stand in between you, waiting and wanting to be called so that it can comply. Once this exercise is performed reliably and with control in the house or garden, practise it in a quiet, enclosed park.

Below The second person calls, runs backwards, then praises and rewards the dog as before.

Right The second person should then stand up and ignore the dog while the first person calls again. Only do this a couple of times each session to prevent boredom.

USING A TRAILING LONG LINE

A long line is simply string or cord, strong enough to take the weight of your dog when it is running and about 30 metres (30 yards) long. The line should have a clip at one end to attach to the dog's collar. A long line can be a useful tool in recall training, as it enables you to demonstrate your effective control to your dog, even at a distance.

1 THE LONG LINE IS TRAILED ALONG THE GROUND BEHIND THE DOG. It can be trodden on to slow or stop the dog if necessary. This enables you to give the dog the impression of freedom, while still retaining control. For the sake of your hands, do not hold or pick up a running line, as you will suffer rope burns. Place your foot on it instead.

2 IF YOUR DOG IGNORES YOU, STEP ON THE LINE AND CALL IT ONCE MORE. Try to do this just before the line becomes taut, but be careful not to snag the dog's (or any bystander's) legs. Your dog will slowly come to a halt. If it still doesn't come to you, tug on the line and run backwards to cue it into its earlier training.

3 ALWAYS REWARD AND PRAISE THE DOG ENTHUSIASTICALLY. Do this every time the dog turns and comes to you,

even if you had to use the line to make it come back each time.

4 AFTER SEVERAL EXPERIENCES LIKE THIS, YOUR PUPPY SHOULD LEARN THAT YOU CAN CONTROL IT AT A DISTANCE. Once you are confident that your puppy is returning more reliably, you can gradually cut the length of the line (so the pup doesn't notice it disappearing), then get rid of it.

5 TRY NOT TO USE A SPRING-LOADED EXTENDING LEAD. This type of lead is often too short to be of any real use. It can trip up other dogs and park users, and it is too obvious to the dog to be of any great training assistance.

PAWS FOR THOUGHT

Using the long line gives you a broader zone of comfort within which to teach your recall lessons. It removes the panic factor. There should be no embarrassing vignettes of you running after your dog waving your arms wildly and futilely shouting yourself hoarse. The long line also allows your dog to mix normally with other dogs in the park and learn essential social skills, while you can remain in control with your soignée reputation intact.

RECALL TIPS

Don't desensitize your dog to its name by using it aimlessly or in vain. Only call your puppy when it counts for something. This will prevent the dog from becoming immune to the sound of its name.

Save your best table scraps and freeze them, so that you have the very best food rewards available at the touch of a defrost button. Carry a variety of these (defrosted) treats in a little plastic pot or a plastic bag – otherwise your dog might chew on your pocket linings when you're not looking.

Routinely run away from your dog whenever you call it to you, even if only for a few steps. This should elicit an even better recall response. Running across a dog's field of vision grabs its attention much better than running directly away from it. You can slow down after it starts to run after you. When it gets close to you, turn to face it, offer it its treats or toy, all the while continuing to walk backwards away from it. Always get a firm hold of the collar before giving your dog the reward.

Walking the same predictable route allows some dogs to become overconfident and venture too far away. You may find that changing directions without warning or perhaps zigzagging unpredictably will teach your puppy to keep a closer check on you.

If your dog is lazy about coming back on recall, it may be useful to dart behind a tree or bush surreptitiously, and hide until the dog notices you are missing. Remain there and let it panic very slightly, then call it and run across its field of vision to prompt it into running to you before it runs off in the wrong direction. Make it think it only just caught you in time; you want it to believe that it can't just dawdle back to you. Do this enough to teach it to keep an eye on you, but don't overdo it or the dog will become neurotic and never leave your side.

Don't chastise your puppy when it comes back to you, no matter how 'bad' it has been or how long it has taken you to catch it. You are only giving it a valid reason to stay away, and it will be even harder to catch next time. If you want to do something constructive, practise a little recall training on the lead and the long line every day, until the dog has improved.

Never call your dog for anything that it may not like, such as punishment, grooming, nail clipping or bathing.

Until you have a reliable recall, avoid making a game of chasing your puppy

Right Use whatever reward your dog likes best. The more tempting it is, the greater its success.

(especially after calling it) while it runs away from you, as this could create problems later on. Ignore it if it tosses a toy at you and then stands back for you to throw or kick it for them. Refer to page 130 for more about games.

Do not make your puppy sit before rewarding it. If you do, you won't be rewarding the most important part of the exercise: the recall. Once the dog is coming reliably, reward it for the recall first, then ask it to sit for a bonus treat.

TEACHING THE DOWN AND SIT

Choose a reward appropriate to your dog. Some dogs would sell their soul for a tasty treat, while others prefer to work for a toy. Toys work best when the dog is feeling playful, while food works best if the dog is greedy or hungry. Some dogs are happy with either approach, so be flexible and take advantage of the circumstances.

Only teach one position – either the 'down' or the 'sit' – at a time, otherwise you will only confuse your dog. The down is generally more difficult to teach than the sit position, so it is a good idea to teach the down properly first.

As with all new exercises, these should ideally be taught in a non-distracting environment at first, and once the dog has the basic idea, he can progress to learning in different environments, and under increasing levels of distraction.

Right Always teach the down position from the stand to prevent any possibility of confusion with the sit.

THE DOWN POSITION

1 HAVE SOME IRRESISTIBLE TREATS IN YOUR RIGHT HAND. Kneel facing the dog's right side, and start with the dog standing.

2 TOUCH THE DOG'S NOSE WITH YOUR RIGHT HAND. Hold the treats very still in a loose fist. The dog should sniff or nibble at your fingers. While its attention is focussed on your right hand, gently rest the flat of your left hand on its shoulder blades, lightly hooking your thumb over its collar.

3 MOVE YOUR TREAT HAND VERY SLOWLY FROM THE PUPPY'S NOSE DOWN TO ITS TOES.

Your hand ends up resting on the floor, just behind the dog's front toes. As it follows the treats with its nose, it will start to lower itself. Once its nose reaches the ground, slide the treat toward the dog's chest, until it is level with the 'wrists' of its front feet. The dog should go into a play bow position with its chest on the ground and its bottom in the air (see right).

4 SOME DOGS MOVE INTO THE DOWN ON THEIR OWN AT THIS POINT. If your dog is stuck in the play bow position, help it to complete the down movement by applying gentle backward and downward pressure on the shoulders, toward the hind feet. The dog should learn to recognize the physical reinforcement (the push), as well as the hand signal (the lure). Don't slide your hand down its back; you may put pressure on the wrong place and hurt it.

5 SAY 'GOOD DOWN' SEVERAL TIMES ONCE YOUR DOG IS IN THE DOWN POSITION. Reward it by loosening your right hand and letting it take a treat or two. Praise the dog verbally, but try not to pat it or rub it too vigorously, or it may try to rise before you want it to. Keep your right hand at ground level by its wrists, and keep dispensing treats intermittently to keep the dog settled in the down.

Left Slowly move the treat down to the floor or ground, between the dog's 'wrists'.

you are using one: put it away rather than leaving it with the dog for it to continue playing with.

8 AFTER A WEEK OR TWO, BEGIN PHASING OUT THE FOOD REWARDS. Start by giving a reward for lying down. While the dog is munching on its treat, take your treat hand away from under its nose, and hide it behind your back briefly before giving out another treat. Keep your free hand on its collar at the back of its neck, in case it tries to rise. Bring back the treat hand almost immediately, and give the dog a 'bonus' reward for its patience. As it grasps the principle, you can keep the food hand away for longer periods. Progress to making the dog wait until you

6 ALLOW IT TO RISE FROM THE EXERCISE BY GIVING IT A RELEASE COMMAND. Move your treat hand away at the same time. The dog will soon understand it has to wait until given permission to move.

7 REPEAT THIS LITTLE AND OFTEN. Two or three times in each session is ideal, but no more than that. A good tip is never to give away all the treats. If you walk away with some still in your hand, your dog will finish each session keen for more training. Do the same thing with the toy if

COMMON MISTAKES TO AVOID WHEN TRAINING THE DOWN POSITION
● Be careful not to say 'sit down'. This is a major source of confusion for dogs, as they do not know which command to obey. As we all know, it is impossible to 'sit' and 'down' at the same time.
● Avoid confusing your dog by using the down command when you mean other things, such as getting off the furniture or jumping up at people. In these cases, always employ a different command – something simple such as 'get off' is ideal.
● If your dog doesn't like your hand touching its collar, don't force the issue. Change to luring it under a low barrier such as a chair leg or low table, so that it has to assume the down position in order to reach the reward.

have stood up before dispensing further treats. Then ask for a down before showing the dog the food, so that the food is a reward rather than a bribe. Remind your puppy by gently pressing him into the down, before producing the treats.

Left Praise and reward your dog when it is still in the down position.

THE SIT POSITION

1 THERE IS ONE VERY EASY WAY TO TEACH YOUR DOG THE SIT POSITION. Simply hold a toy or treat just above its head and move the lure backwards, just out of reach. The dog should look up as the lure moves back over its head and sit down of its own accord.

2 OR TRY THIS WAY TO MAKE YOUR DOG SIT. Gently pull back (not up) on the collar with one hand, with the other hand at the shoulder blades. Slowly slide the hand down the back and gently press on the dog's hind quarters, just above its tail.

Above Slide one hand from the dog's shoulders down its back to its hips, while holding the dog's collar with your other hand.

Right Gently pull back the collar, while also gently pressing down on the dog's hips.

3 TRY NOT TO SAY THE WORD 'SIT'.
During the early training sessions, wait until the dog has assumed the position, or you may teach it the wrong association. Say 'good sit' a few times when it does eventually sit, then give it the reward and make a fuss over it. Do this two or three times in a session, with several sessions a day, and your puppy will soon understand the meaning of the word. Only once this has happened can you begin using the 'sit' command as a prompt to sit.

Below Once the dog is in the sit position, repeat the phrase 'good sit' several times.

TITBIT
Do not have food in your hands if you are handling your dog into the sit position, or it will struggle to reach it. Reward your puppy or dog by gently stroking its back or scratching it under the chin, but keep it there briefly. Make certain that it is relaxed before you allow it to rise out of the sit position by giving it its release command.

THE RELEASE COMMAND
Every time you ask a dog to do something, you should clearly signal the end of that exercise with a release command or phrase such as 'that will do' or 'off you go'. Move the dog out of position as you say the command, and it will eventually come to understand that it can go 'off duty' when it hears those words.

Do not use 'OK' or 'come on' as release commands, as these are commonly spoken phrases that could easily confuse the dog.

THE SIT AND DOWN STAYS

Once your dog has learnt how to sit and lie down on command, you may wish to teach it to stay longer in that position. This exercise can be very useful in a wide variety of situations, such as when you answer the front door, in the vet's waiting room, or if you need your dog to remain in the background temporarily while you deal with something else.

'Stays' are best taught by gradually increasing the amount of time and distance before you return to release the dog. You should reward your dog intermittently (with praise or food) throughout the 'stay'. Always return to stand next to your dog, and make a big fuss of it before releasing it. This should prevent it from anticipating your release command prematurely. Consistently use a release command (phrase or signal) to mark the point when the dog can get up and 'break' the exercise. No reward should be given after the dog has risen. This makes it very clear to the dog that compliance is the key to the rewards.

If the dog does rise prematurely, the reward should be visibly removed from the dog's sight, and the dog placed back in its original position. The rewards are only reintroduced and given again once the dog is in the correct place and position.

COMMON MISTAKES TO AVOID WHEN TRAINING THE STAYS

• Don't train the sit and the down stays in the same session or you may confuse your dog. If you give it too many things to remember at once, it will end up metaphorically chasing its tail.

• Don't use the 'stay' command for both the sit and the down stay – how is it supposed to know which one you mean? In any case, you shouldn't really need a stay command if your dog has been correctly taught to maintain any given position until told otherwise (with the consistent use of a release command).

• Some owners inadvertently make more of a fuss of their dogs after they finish the exercise than they do during the actual exercise itself. This can cause dogs to anticipate the extra reward and encourage them to rise before they should. If a release

Left A reliable sit stay can prove extremely useful in a variety of everyday situations.

command is correctly used, it allows you to reward and praise the dog sufficiently during the exercise without tempting it to break prematurely.

Never nag your dog during a stay by wagging your finger at it, sending it threatening looks or repeating commands excessively. Where dogs have been forced and bullied into staying, the results tend to be much less reliable. This is because dogs do not learn so well under stress. If the dog doesn't enjoy the exercise, it will always be on the lookout for ways to get out of doing it. Wouldn't you?

Teach your dog by lavishing it with lots of verbal praise (and occasional food reinforcement) while it is in the sit or down position. Make a big fuss of the dog on your return while keeping it in position, and then give the release command. Immediately after, you should stop playing and almost ignore the dog by comparison. Your precious pooch will bask in the glory of being such a goody-goody and care significantly less about getting up from its position.

Never leave your dog in a stay position outside a store or anywhere it could cause an accident or be hurt, lost or stolen, even if you'll only be gone for an instant. You wouldn't treat your child like this so don't do it to your faithful canine.

THE STAND FOR VETERINARY EXAMINATION

It may not seem an obvious goal, but it is vital that your dog learns to be tolerant of being gently restrained and examined in the stand position. This useful exercise prepares your dog for what to expect when it visits the veterinary surgery.

1 HOLD THE DOG'S COLLAR AT THE NAPE OF ITS NECK WITH YOUR RIGHT HAND. Support its stomach with your left forearm. All you want is for your dog to stand still for a few seconds while you praise it, then use your release command and let go of it. The dog's passport to release is to conform.

2 RESIST THE TEMPTATION TO FUSS IF IT WRIGGLES OR STRUGGLES. If this happens, ignore it, but do not let go of the dog until it has tired itself out and stopped for a breather.

Right It is very important that your dog becomes accustomed to being lifted onto a table and being gently restrained and examined – while at the vet's, for instance.

When it stops struggling, praise and release it immediately.

3 ALLOW THE DOG TO BECOME USED TO BEING EXAMINED BY SOMEONE ELSE. At first, the 'examiner' should be a family member, then you can ask a friend to help. The examiner should give treats intermittently from one hand while running the other hand over the dog. Your vet will thank you for teaching this. More importantly, your dog will learn to relax and tolerate being examined.

FURTHER TRAINING

Now that you and your puppy have mastered the basics, it is time to build on the training that you have already done. Going out of the front door, teaching control at the front door, walking on a loose lead, dealing with confirmed 'pullers', common problems, training aids and teaching the 'settle on your mat' are all handy but essential things that will produce a dog you can be proud of and one that is the envy of all your friends and neighbours.

GOING OUT OF THE FRONT DOOR

The front door is often the site of some very excitable and uncontrolled behaviour. Some dogs become so overexcited that they wind themselves up to fever pitch at the prospect of going out and behave like 'lager louts' or juvenile delinquents, pushing past their owners and dragging them out of the front door and down the street at top speed.

Owners who permit or even encourage their dog to become overstimulated often unwittingly train in this wild behaviour. This appalling display of bad manners is then rewarded with a walk. No wonder so many dogs are reluctant to give up what they perceive to be a successful form of behaviour, especially one that has worked so reliably and predictably in the past.

To counter this behaviour, you need to stop rewarding it. Doorway control is best taught initially as a separate exercise, then incorporated into going out for a walk Otherwise the prospect of going out for a walk can be simply too exhilarating for your dog and distract it from learning.

TEACHING CONTROL AT THE FRONT DOOR

1 MAKE YOUR DOG SIT IN THE SAME SPOT BY THE FRONT DOOR TO HAVE ITS LEAD ATTACHED. If it won't comply, put the lead away, abandon the walk (if you were going for one) and try again later. This will allow your dog to learn from its mistakes, as well as its successes.

2 DO THIS EXERCISE THROUGHOUT THE DAY AFTER YOUR DOG HAS HAD ITS MORNING EXERCISE. This will cut down on the guilt factor if you find yourself wanting to cave in at the soulful look in those melting brown eyes. The more you practise, the easier it gets, so persevere.

Left Teach your dog good manners, so that it doesn't rush out the front door ahead of you.

3 ATTACH THE DOG'S LEAD, THEN MAKE THE DOG SIT STILL WHILE YOU OPEN THE FRONT DOOR. This can take time – and patience – to teach, but is worth the effort.

4 STEP OVER THE THRESHOLD WHILE THE DOG REMAINS SITTING. Move very slowly when introducing this stage, and try to keep the dog very calm and focused. Each time your dog waits on the inside, it should be rewarded with praise and a tasty treat. If it tries to rise and cross the threshold before being told, put it back into the sit position exactly where it was before. Keep doing this until it gives in and waits obediently.

5 ALWAYS STOP FOR A SIGNIFICANT PAUSE BEFORE YOU CALL THE DOG OVER THE THRESHOLD TO YOU. Then make it sit next to you while you lock up. The more you practise this, the quicker your dog will learn that bad behaviour backfires by delaying its walk, whereas good behaviour is rewarded and will move it closer to its goal – the outside world. Stick to this plan consistently, and the dog should become less excited and more compliant.

Left The sight of your dog waiting patiently at the front door is very pleasing once it is achieved.

**1 BEGIN TRAINING IN A QUIET AND
FAMILIAR ENVIRONMENT.** Your garden,
backyard or house are all ideal. The dog
should be wearing a good-quality nylon
collar with a metal buckle. A plastic clip
is more prone to breaking. Do not use a
leather collar as it may break, and never
use a check chain as you could hurt your
dog. Make sure the collar is tight enough
that it cannot be pulled over your dog's
head. Use a comfortable but strong lead
about 1 metre (3 feet) long. Braid or leather
leads are best for this; do not use a chain
lead as it could easily hurt your hands.

**2 START BY STANDING STILL, LURING AND
COAXING YOUR DOG INTO THE CORRECT
POSITION.** This is by your side and close
to your leg. Give it a tasty treat, and praise
it when it reaches you. Dispense the treats
from the hand nearest the dog, otherwise
it will cross in front of you to reach your
other hand and trip you up. Always offer
the reward as near to the side of your leg
as possible, as this will encourage the
dog to maintain that position. Make
certain that the lead is loose.

WALKING ON A
LOOSE LEAD

Left to their own devices, most dogs will
tend to drag their owners around, half
strangling themselves in the process. They
need to be taught to walk properly on the
lead without pulling, stopping or darting
off suddenly. The object of the exercise
is to teach your dog that it can walk
anywhere within the full extent of the lead,
on either side of you, as long as it doesn't
try to pull beyond the extent of the lead
and make it taut. Pulling on the lead
should be shown to be counterproductive,
while walking close to your leg should be
seen as highly rewarding.

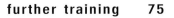

Left and below Use the lead and some treats to encourage the dog into the right position and lure it forwards, one step at a time.

this until you are able to walk slowly and deliberately, varying the number of paces between stops. Chat to the dog when it is not pulling, and give it tasty treats to reward good behaviour. Always stop to let the dog eat the treat before setting off again. Stop and reward it frequently while it is learning the correct position, then you can progress by making the dog work a little bit longer between the treats.

5 IF THE DOG PULLS TO THE END OF THE LEAD, USE THE LEAD TO REPOSITION IT. Then touch the food to its nose, or lure it into the correct position, rewarding it when it gets there. You may need to do this a lot before your dog gets the idea.

6 YOUR DOG MAY BE OVERKEEN AND JUMP UP OR SNATCH AT THE TREATS IN YOUR HAND. If this is the case, accelerate slightly until it walks normally for a few steps, then you can stop and reward it.

3 ONCE THE DOG HAS GRASPED THE CONCEPT AT A STANDSTILL, YOU CAN PROGRESS TO MOVING. Take one step forward before stopping, and correct the dog's position if it pulls to the end of the lead. Reward it when it stops with you in the correct position.

4 WHEN THE DOG STARTS AND STOPS WITH YOU ONE STEP AT A TIME, PROGRESS TO TWO STEPS. Continue like

7 IF YOUR DOG IS NOT INTERESTED IN KEEPING UP WITH YOU, SLOW DOWN AND BE MORE OBVIOUS WITH THE LURE. It may be you need to offer better treats – I find that real meat and fish scraps work far better than store-bought treats. It could also be you are asking for too much before rewarding, so try rewarding more often, or work with less distractions.

you – stealth is the key. The dog learns this is a consequence of that particular behaviour and it should be deterred. Biting at your clothes can be an attention-seeking ploy, so it is vital that you appear detached and disinterested as you mete out the secret punishment.

SCAVENGING?

Make sure that you do not drop any treats on the floor, as this will simply teach your dog to scavenge.

SNIFFING AND LEG LIFTING AT EVERY LAMP-POST AND TREE?

Most male (and some female) dogs like to stop and sniff at every opportunity and cock their legs to 'urine mark' territory, but you shouldn't allow your dog to pull you from pillar to post. Only permit it to stop and urinate (while on the lead) with your express permission, by saying its cue command learnt during toilet training (see pages 34–5). If you walk the dog briskly past all the remaining trees and lamp-posts, your walks will be much more pleasant. Needless to say, the dog can cock its leg to its heart's content when it is running freely in the park off its lead.

PROBLEMS AND HOW TO DEAL WITH THEM

TOO DISTRACTED?

If your dog is distracted and unswayed by treats, you may need to spend more time socializing it to allow it to become familiar with the environment. In the meantime, carry out your training sessions in a less distracting place. Once your dog is used to the distractions, you can introduce them into your training.

CHEWING THE LEAD?

If your dog likes to chew the lead as you're walking along, try temporarily using a chain lead, as this usually puts off even the most determined chompers.

BITING AT CLOTHING?

If your dog bites at your clothing, squirt it surreptitiously with some water from a concealed plastic lemon juice dispenser (see page 48). Be casual about this, so the dog does not realize that it comes from

THROWING A PAW OVER THE LEAD?

If done repeatedly, this is often a trick for attention. Ignore it for as long as possible. Walk on for a few paces before untangling the dog with the minimum of fuss.

WON'T WALK?

This could be the result of fear or your dog could be trying to dictate to you. In either case, seek professional help.

MEETING OTHER DOGS ON LEAD?

Slacken off the lead, so that your dog can move and express itself properly. Freedom of movement allows dogs to communicate properly; a tight lead often causes an unnecessary fight.

CHASING AFTER TRAFFIC?

Chasing moving vehicles can obviously be fatal, or at the very least it may lead to distressing injuries and expensive vet's bills, so seek specialist help without delay.

PULLING TOWARDS OR JUMPING UP AT PEOPLE IN THE STREET?

Most puppies go through this stage until they learn better. In the meantime, put your dog on the side of you furthest from the approaching person, and shorten the lead as you walk past to keep the dog at bay. Alternatively, stop and make it sit, holding its attention with a treat and a prudent hand in the collar until the person is safely past, then reward the dog.

FAILING TO RESPOND TO THE 'HEEL' COMMAND?

Strictly speaking, the word 'heel' should never have to pass your lips, as your dog should be conditioned never to pull when on its lead. The mere presence of the lead should be a clear signal to behave.

PULLING REPEATEDLY?

This often happens with extending leads as it wrongly teaches a dog that pulling gets results. Try changing to a good leather or braid lead for better control.

Left Keep all training sessions short so that your dog doesn't become tired or bored.

CONFIRMED PULLERS

Older dogs with very bad habits firmly ingrained may not respond to 'food luring', in which case you may need to introduce another type of consequence as a reaction to your dog's pulling on its lead.

Try taking several steps backwards each time the dog tries to pull ahead, then use the lead to manoeuvre the dog in to the desired position. Then loosen the lead, reward, and proceed forward again. If that doesn't work, you could also try one of the following: stopping dead in your tracks; changing direction without any warning, or stopping and making the dog sit next to you; or only offering a reward when the dog adopts the right position, whether this is by accident or design.

Let your dog use its intelligence to work things out for itself. Its experiences will teach it that every time it pulls on the lead, this makes you stop or change direction. The only way for it to know where you are going is to stay far enough back to keep one eye on you. This, of course, is impossible to do if it is in front with its back to you, so it will learn to keep back in a more adaptable position.

In the beginning, you may have to correct so often that you do not make any progress in the desired direction. Don't worry – the more you chop and change

Left Who's leading whom? Allowing your dog to pull on its lead when it is young can seriously backfire later.

without warning, the quicker the dog will learn. It is important to break the dog's eye contact with whatever it was pulling towards, so you may have to turn away from the distraction before being able to divert its attention back to you.

Don't command or warn your dog, as you want it to use its eyes rather than responding to your voice to avoid being caught out, thereby necessitating the need for it to drop back into a better viewing position – which is, after all, the whole point of the exercise.

Once the dog has grasped the general idea, you can correct it and still achieve

forward progress by doing an about-turn with only a few steps in the opposite direction before turning back to go in the original direction again. Later you can make a double about-turn if the dog goes to pull on its lead, making it walk all the way around you before proceeding.

By now, the dog should be paying more attention to what you are doing to avoid being caught out. It may require an occasional reminder, but most of your pulling problems – not to mention the dog itself – should be behind you.

TITBIT

There are lots of anti-pulling training aids on the market that claim to help you control or correct pulling on the lead. Some are better than others, and the best can be very useful if you have a dog that is too strong for you. Further details of these are on page 120.

TEACH THE 'SETTLE' OR 'ON YOUR MAT'

THE OVERALL OBJECTIVE

The aim is to teach the dog to go to a marked area – in this case a moveable mat or dog towel – and settle down on it, wherever you happen to be.

WHY YOU SHOULD TEACH THIS EXERCISE

The settle is very useful for controlling your dog in all sorts of situations – at the vet's, when visiting friends, in a bar or other public areas, or wherever and whenever you would prefer your dog to settle down calmly in one place.

This exercise gives your dog a kind of 'security blanket' that can travel around with it. Use something washable and easy to carry, such as a dog towel, rather than the dog's actual bed.

There are two components to this exercise: the 'send to' the towel and the 'lie down' at the end. These are initially taught separately, then combined later.

WHAT YOU NEED TO TRAIN THIS EXERCISE

- Your dog's favourite treats
- Collar and lead
- A dog towel or washable mat

- A happy and reliable 'down' response from your dog (see pages 64–5)

WHICH CUE WORDS TO USE

The phrases 'on your mat' or 'go and settle' seem to work consistently well. This is not the same exercise as your dog being sent to its bed. The mat is far more versatile (and portable), so these two objectives must have clearly different cue words to avoid any confusion.

WHEN TO TRAIN

This exercise can be done at your convenience, but it must be carried out at least two or three times a day for the first week or two. It pays to introduce this exercise when the dog is slightly hungry and when there are few distractions, so pick a quiet time just before its mealtime. Only once the dog has become familiar with the exercise can you

Right Teaching your dog to settle can prove useful when you need it to stay put.

start to allow mild and (later on) stronger distractions to improve reliability.

WHERE TO TRAIN THIS EXERCISE

Use a different place each time you train this command. Start by using various places in the house, then progress to different parts of the garden or backyard, all your friends' houses, the vet's and so on. The more places you practise this command, the better at it your dog will become.

1 LAY A MAT OR DOG TOWEL ON THE GROUND. Drop a few treats in the centre of the mat (without allowing your dog to see) and bring your dog close to the mat (on its collar and lead). Let it hover near the towel until it discovers the treats there. Say 'on your mat' a few times as it eats the treats. Drop some more treats on the mat for it to find, again saying 'on your mat' as it helps itself. Do not make the dog lie down on the towel at all in steps 1–4. The down position should be taught separately (see pages 64–5) and only introduced when it is

reliable, at step 5. Repeat this stage a couple of times before proceeding.

2 LET THE DOG SEE A TREAT ON THE MAT. This time, use the lead to allow the dog to draw near the treat, but restrain it close enough so that it is not able to eat it. Next slowly drag the dog away from the treat and a little way off the mat, saying 'off you go' (this will later be the release phrase that gives the dog permission to get off the mat). At this point, the dog should be desperate to pull back to the mat (and the treat). You don't want to discourage the dog, so don't correct or chastise it.

3 ALMOST IMMEDIATELY, SLACKEN THE PRESSURE ON THE LEAD. Allow the dog to pull back to the mat. At this point, you should keep saying 'on your mat' the entire time the dog is pulling towards it and eating the treats.

4 FINISH THE SESSION BY DRAGGING THE DOG AWAY FROM A TREAT. Fold the mat up in front of your dog so that it will remember that a treat was left in there. Your dog will be even keener next time you bring out the mat.

Above Drop the treats on the mat for your dog to find.

Right Let your dog lead you to the mat, and give the command is it retrieves the reward.

Above Once your dog understands, coax it into the down position for a bonus treat.

This is a sort of canine variation on the old adage that the way to a man's heart is through his stomach – only in this case it is compliance you are seeking.

Repeat steps 1 to 4 until your dog is reliably keen on pulling towards the mat. When you also have a reliable down response, you can join this onto the end of the exercise as follows.

5 ONLY PUT ONE TREAT ON THE MAT. Send the dog to the mat, and let it eat the treat and look over the mat. Once your dog is satisfied that there are no further treats on the mat, you can ask it to lie down. When it does so, give it a bonus treat.

Continue this until the dog begins to predict the routine and lies down after eating the first treat, ready for the second.

6 SEND YOUR DOG TO AN EMPTY (TREATLESS) MAT, ASK FOR A DOWN, THEN REWARD IT. Repeat this stage until the dog is going to the mat and lying down straightaway for its treat.

7 KEEP YOUR DOG LYING IN THE DOWN POSITION ON THE MAT FOR PROGRESSIVELY LONGER PERIODS. Reward the dog intermittently, and try to encourage it to settle there for a few minutes at a time.

Below Help the dog into the down position if necessary.

Above Give the dog a further treat for lying down on its mat.

TRAINING TIPS

- Always practise this exercise on the lead, so that you can easily and readily control the dog's movements.
- Make sure the dog is pulling you to the mat and not the other way around.
- During the early training stages, only say the phrase 'on your mat' at the precise moment the dog is rewarding itself from the mat. This helps to build up the correct word association.
- Don't let the dog see you drop the treats on the mat. You want it to believe that this is a magic carpet that sprouts treats, so wait until it is looking down or away from the mat before dropping the treats. This will teach your dog to focus on the mat rather than on you.
- If any treats bounce off or land outside the mat, pick them up before your dog does. It must only receive treats from the mat itself.
- Ensure that your dog's 'down' response is reliable before you ask the dog to lie down on its mat – if not, practise the 'down' separately (not as part of this exercise) until the dog is willingly responding.
- Never use this exercise as a punishment, as you will deter your dog from complying in the future.

6 WALKIES!

All dogs need exercise – even the little ones. Whatever your breed of dog, it will need to exercise its mind and its body on a regular basis, regardless of rain, hail, sleet, snow, or shine. You'll need to know how much exercise is appropriate, how to introduce your puppy to going 'off lead' in the park and how to socialize it with dogs it meets on its journeys.

WHAT TYPE OF EXERCISE AND HOW MUCH?

Most dogs were bred to do a job, so they will require a significant amount of activity and exercise to take the place of what would have been their 'work'. Size has nothing to do with it – some small dogs are the busiest and require more activity than larger 'couch potato' type dogs.

Below Regular exercise is vital for all dogs, irrespective of size or breed, or even their inclination.

All adult dogs require at least 30 to 60 minutes of free running in a safe and secure area, such as a field or a park, every day. Puppies need less (see box). In very hot weather, it is best to wait until the cooler times of the day.

Every dog needs a life away from home, where it can meet and interact normally with its own species, express a wide range of natural behaviours and burn off excess energy.

Time spent in the garden or backyard (no matter how large it is) is no substitute for exploring a new environment each day. Dogs quickly become bored with their own gardens and can get 'cabin fever' if they're not taken out.

Dogs that don't receive appropriate exercise or mental stimulation become frustrated and stressed, and are far more likely to divert those energies into unwanted behavioural problems.

PAWS FOR THOUGHT

Don't overexercise your growing puppy. Until it is fully grown, you should build up its tolerance to exercise gradually. As a rough guide, puppies need about five minutes of exercise for every month of age: at three months, they can go out for 15 minutes at a time; at four months, 20 minutes; and so on. You can take your puppy out for the appropriate length of time twice a day.

Some people try to exercise their puppy to excess in an attempt to tire it out physically and mentally. If you overstimulate and overtire your puppy, you will only make it irritable and hyperactive, which is counterproductive to your original intentions. You can also damage the delicate growth plates of its developing joints, and this can cause permanent lameness.

THE FIRST FEW VISITS TO THE PARK

The first time you take your puppy for a walk in the park, pick a wide, open space, so that it will want to stay near you. There is less likelihood of distractions or cover luring it away. Run away from the puppy quite a bit, encouraging it to chase after you. Give it heaps of attention and tasty treats when it catches up with you. As your puppy becomes more confident,

you could start playing hide and seek behind trees to teach it to keep an eye on you. Make a big game of it, but don't overdo it, or the dog will become neurotic and never leave your side.

You can leave the trailing long line on as a precaution against the unlikely event of it darting off in the opposite direction to you. Actually, it is extremely unlikely that your puppy will try to run away from you, but it will give you tremendous comfort and

confidence knowing that the line is there, just in case something should go awry.

Also, take a favourite toy with you so that your dog thinks that you are fun to be with – otherwise you will find yourself abandoned in favour of other, far more interesting distractions.

Below Regular free-running is essential for a healthy canine mind and body.

MEETING OTHER DOGS

It is essential that your puppy or adult dog mixes with a variety of other dogs regularly (see page 41). Although you may well feel that your precious pooch is a cut above the rest of the pack, there is no room for snobbery here. It is important that it be allowed to play off lead with suitable dogs, as long as the play is not too rough. If your dog is annoying them, or pushing its luck, they will probably cut it down to size – not literally, of course – and that should teach your hound better manners for next time. If it is not improving with each experience, consult a dog trainer before your dog causes a fight.

Do not restrain your dog on a leash or extending lead when it is trying to interact with other dogs, because they could become tangled up or accidentally give the wrong signals to each other, something which could all too easily lead to a fight. If you do not trust your dog to come back to you, run it on a trailing line (see page 62) and teach it better recalls (see pages 58–63).

If you walk your dog in popular areas at popular times, you are less likely to meet aggressive dogs, as their owners try to avoid trouble wherever possible. If you do meet an unfriendly-looking dog on your walk, try not to panic, pull your dog away or pick it up, as you may simply escalate

Above Socializing with other dogs is an essential aspect of a puppy's development. It helps to teach the dog its place in the order of things.

the situation. If you are unsure, ask the other dog's owner before the dogs meet.

Always keep your dog on its lead when walking on the street or near roads. It is neither smart nor safe to walk your dog off its lead near traffic; many dogs are injured or killed in this way. You certainly wouldn't want your dog to be unexpectedly distracted by something and run under the wheels of a car.

Only let your dog off lead in the park if you are in complete control of it. It must return to you reliably when called. See the section on recall training on pages 58–63.

Below It is important to make sure your dog is sociable, particularly when it comes to other dogs, so allow it to mix with them on a regular basis.

PAWS FOR THOUGHT

- Use your discretion. Timid dogs and dogs that are very old or very young are best protected from overenthusiastic dogs and young puppies, but should be fine with calmer ones.
- Owners who walk their dogs in the park but keep them on their leads could be doing so for all sorts of reasons, so keep your dog away. Even dogs that are normally fine with other dogs when running free can suddenly become aggressive towards those same dogs when back on the lead. There are many reasons for this, so don't let your dogs mix on short or extending leads.
- Dogs often wear muzzles if they scavenge or are aggressive, so it is wise to keep your dog away from them unless you know for sure.

POOP SCOOP

You are legally obliged to pick up and dispose of your dog's faeces in most places now. Even without the threat of a fine, it is simple courtesy not to leave your dog's droppings all over the place where anyone can step in them. Always carry plastic bags with you whenever you take your dog out.

PAWS FOR THOUGHT

Don't allow your dog to jump about or play when it has just eaten, nor should you exercise, train or walk your dog on a full stomach. Physical activity combined with a full stomach can cause a life-threatening condition known as stomach torsion or bloat (see page 105).

TITBIT

Dogs that are walked regularly in wooded areas or allowed to chase birds and small animals such as squirrels will soon aspire to be professional hunters. They will often ignore their owners in favour of a chase, which then progresses to going briefly out of sight. As they become more practised and bolder, they tend to disappear for longer periods, until it reaches the point where you lose them altogether.

This can be a really difficult problem to train your dog out of. To prevent this from happening, you need to develop and teach your dog a better game – one that involves you, rather than excludes you.

PUBERTY AND SEXUAL BEHAVIOUR

The onset of puberty normally occurs between six and 12 months of age, although occasionally it takes place earlier or later. Adolescence and its associated hormonal changes can drastically alter your dog's behaviour and attitude. It is therefore important to know how to recognize the onset of puberty, what to expect and how to manage those changes successfully. You will also need to decide whether and when to neuter your dog, so it is wise to be well informed of all of the considerations.

MALE ADOLESCENCE AND SEXUAL BEHAVIOUR

The onset of puberty can cause several changes in your dog's behaviour. As his testosterone levels rise, he will start to cock his leg when he urinates. He will become much more interested in sniffing and scent marking, and much more likely to roam further away from you. He may be increasingly distracted by other dogs, more independent and less obedient.

While most male dogs cope reasonably well with puberty and continue to behave acceptably with dogs and people, some dogs are so adversely affected that they deteriorate rapidly into rampant or aggressive behaviour, transforming them from Bambi to Rambo practically overnight.

POTENTIAL PROBLEMS

DOG DISTRACTION AND DISOBEDIENCE

If your previously obedient puppy becomes excessively independent or distracted by other dogs, to the point where you can no longer control him easily on walks, you should have him neutered without delay. Don't wince at the thought. If you wait too long, he will only fall into bad habits that will be much harder to overcome.

SEXUAL FRUSTRATION

Mounting behaviour directed towards people, dogs or almost anything is not necessarily sexually motivated (see page 52). Elevated hormone levels are the likely culprit if this behaviour first appears or significantly increases at the onset of leg cocking, in which case neutering should alleviate the problem considerably.

Some dogs become obsessive about crotch sniffing or can become sexually stimulated by the faintest scent of blood – normally a bitch in season locally, but sometimes even a woman menstruating or a cut finger. Their eyes glaze over, their lower jaw judders and they start salivating. Their brain 'addles' and they are almost

Left Puberty – from playful puppy to rampant warrior in an instant.

Above Adolescent males may become more competitive.

impossible to get through to – once again, neutering is the answer. Allowing your dog to mate with a bitch will only make the problem worse, rather than better, so this is not a viable solution.

SCENT (URINE) MARKING INDOORS AND OUTDOORS

If your dog starts to lift his leg indoors, neutering will help to solve this. However, whatever you do, don't wait until it has become a habit or it will be difficult to stamp out. Do not allow your dog to drag you from pillar to post to sniff and urine mark when he is on his lead. Keep him on the move and only allow him to stop, sniff and urinate occasionally, and only then with your permission. Use your cue word as taught during toilet training (see pages 34–5).

DOMINANT OR AGGRESSIVE BEHAVIOUR

Adolescent dogs can suddenly become very macho and behave in a pushy or aggressive fashion towards other male dogs – and sometimes people. Again, neutering should help, but it will be less effective if you wait too long to do it or allow the aggression to become an established habit.

UNDESCENDED TESTICLES (CHRYPTORCHIDISM)

This is where one (or less commonly both) of the testicles has not descended properly into the scrotum. The undescended testicle is retained within the abdomen or the inguinal region. If the testicle has not descended properly by the time your dog is six months old, it is unlikely to ever do so.

Chryptorchid dogs can be harder to train, and they are also more prone to problem behaviour. Once again, neutering seems to help. Furthermore, undescended testicles are extremely prone to becoming cancerous, so it is important that they be identified and surgically removed as soon as possible. The normally descended testicle must also be removed, as cryptorchid dogs should never be used for breeding.

NEUTERING (SURGICAL CASTRATION)

Neutering significantly reduces testosterone levels, making male dogs much easier to live with and manage.

Neutered males are less prone to sexual or aggressive behaviour, less likely to ignore you when socializing with other dogs, far easier to train and significantly less likely to instigate dog fights or be picked on by other macho Brutuses.

Neutered males are also far less likely to scent mark indoors and out, and they are much less obsessive about stopping to sniff at everything outside. Neutering also prevents accidental matings and unwanted litters. Neutered dogs are also healthier than their uncastrated counterparts, as castration removes the potential for testicular cancer, prostatitis and anal adenomas.

Neutering a male dog is a relatively simple operation. The dog is anaesthetized, and both testicles are removed through a small incision in the scrotum, which is then closed with sutures. Most dogs are in and out of the vet's surgery the same day and are fully recovered – with you fully forgiven – the following day.

Make sure that your dog cannot pull out his stitches. He may need close supervision until they are removed (about seven to ten days later) or possibly have to wear a special collar from the vet to prevent this happening.

Early neutering at six to nine months old (just before or at the onset of puberty) can help to prevent many of the problems listed opposite from occurring.

Don't leave neutering too late, as any bad behaviour patterns could become habitual, rendering the neutering less effective. With an older dog, one may have to wait between three to nine months to see the full benefits of neutering, as the male hormones in question can take their time to leave the body. If you cannot wait this long, you can ask your vet to give your dog a hormone injection to counter the existing testosterone, and this can give you a head start while you are waiting for the castration to work.

Castration alone is not an instant cure for everything, but it can be a very effective and powerful tool in reducing hormonally induced behaviours.

Some people worry that castrating their dog will take away its 'personality', but this is not true. You don't need to possess a pair of testicles to have a great personality, as proved by many castrated male dogs, bitches and women.

Most people readily understand that stallions, bulls, rams and even tomcats are far more feisty and troublesome than their castrated counterparts, so it should not prove too difficult to view dogs in the same light.

It is also a myth that castration makes dogs fat or lazy. Normally, too much food and/or too little exercise are the real causes of weight gain. Reducing your dog's food by about 10 percent and giving him adequate exercise should mean that this doesn't become a problem.

All male guide dogs for the blind are castrated at puberty for many of the sound reasons listed above – not least because it prevents them from dragging their visually impaired owners from pillar to post to sniff and scent mark. Neutering does not compromise any aspect of their health or working ability.

Occasionally 'show' breeders try to discourage owners from neutering their pets, as judges sometimes discriminate against a neutered animal in the show ring. If you have no intention of showing or breeding from your dog, this is a totally irrelevant consideration.

The only potential downside of neutering is if your dog has a long and silky smooth coat, like the Afghan hound. There is a small chance that the coat may become slightly fluffy after castration, but other coat types are unaffected.

FEMALE ADOLESCENCE AND SEXUAL BEHAVIOUR

The onset of puberty in bitches (female dogs) normally occurs between six and 12 months, and this is marked by her coming into her first season (on heat). Small breeds normally have their first season at around six months old, while the larger breeds tend to mature later – anything up to around a year old.

Each season lasts three weeks, and this period is when the bitch becomes fertile and receptive to mating. During this time, she will be irresistible to uncastrated male dogs (and vice versa), who will try to mate with her or track her down through her pheromone trail.

Unless she is neutered (spayed), a bitch will come into season every six to nine months for her entire life. There is no such thing as the canine menopause.

SO HOW WILL YOU KNOW WHEN SHE IS IN SEASON?

There are many signs to look out for that let you know when your bitch is in season:

Uncastrated male dogs will begin to show more interest in her and will pay a lot of attention to her nether regions.

She will urinate more frequently (to spread her pheromones around and advertise herself to any prospective suitors). Make sure that you take her into the garden more often, otherwise she may urinate in the house.

Her vulva will enlarge and change position from the underbelly to a prominent position under the anus. She many clean (lick) it a lot more than usual.

As the season progresses, she will appear to 'bleed' or discharge from the vulva, and this discharge can vary from a pale straw colour to a strong red hue. This lasts for a few days before disappearing, but your bitch is not out of season until her vulva has reduced in size again and moved back to its normal position. This will happen about three weeks after the first signs.

WHAT PRECAUTIONS SHOULD BE TAKEN?

Keep your bitch under house arrest for the entire three weeks. Only let her loose in your garden or backyard if it is completely dogproof. Keep her occupied by playing lots of games in your house and garden to tire her out.

Do not take her out for a walk or let her off the lead anywhere in case she comes across a potential mate. Don't think you will be able to intervene and protect her from being mounted, as even

POTENTIAL PROBLEMS

ADOLESCENT BEHAVIOUR

Some bitches become really naughty for a week or two preceding their first season because of the hormonal changes. Thankfully, adolescent behaviour in bitches is very short-lived. They calm down and mature significantly during or after their first season and emerge as a far more emotionally fully-fledged adult as a result.

PHANTOM PREGNANCIES

Bitches quite commonly experience a false or phantom pregnancy about nine weeks after the end of their season. This is because their hormones lead them to believe that they are pregnant, regardless of whether or not they were mated.

At the very least, bitches can become depressed, although this varies with each individual. It is only a temporary change, and she will revert back to normal behaviour once this has passed.

At their worst, phantom pregnancies can be quite a traumatic experience for both the dog and the owners, as they can cause a severe personality change in the bitch. She may try to make a nest (possibly by digging up the carpet or hiding in a dark place) and fill it with a collection of toys that she thinks are her puppies, over which she can become very protective or even aggressive. If this happens, remove

Below A phantom pregnancy can temporarily depress your bitch.

Above Keep your bitch entertained during her season by playing games.

normally docile male dogs can become aggressive if you try to interfere. You and your bitch could be seriously injured.

🐾 Never take her to the park at any time while she is in season, or the local dogs will track her home – you could have amorous four-legged suitors camping (and howling) outside your home for the entire three weeks.

🐾 During her season, your bitch may drop some discharge around your home. It is therefore better to confine her to an area that can be easily cleaned or to cover your carpets and furnishings with dust cloths, rather than put her in a position where you have to nag her all the time.

all her toys (without her seeing) and act in a cheerful and indifferent manner. Make allowances for her behaviour and don't punish her for her actions.

In extreme instances, she can actually start producing milk. If this happens, don't stroke her tummy: this stimulates further milk production. Your vet can treat this. Have her spayed as soon as she is fully recovered, as this is likely to recur after her next season, and the condition has a tendency to worsen each time.

WOMB INFECTIONS

Unspayed bitches are prone to developing a pyometra, which is a pus-filled infected womb. This potentially fatal condition requires immediate veterinary treatment. Spaying prevents it.

PREGNANCY

Pregnancy carries many potential problems too numerous to mention here. If your bitch is accidentally mated, take her to your vet immediately for the dog equivalent of the 'morning-after pill'.

MAMMARY (BREAST) TUMOURS

Mammary tumours are far more common in unspayed bitches. Early spaying (before the first season) is believed to prevent mammary tumours completely.

NEUTERING (SPAYING)

Spaying is an operation to surgically remove the ovaries and womb. It is done under anaesthetic and your bitch will have stitches for a least 10 days. You must ensure that she can't pull her stitches out, so she may need close supervision or have to wear a special collar from the vet.

Spayed bitches are spared the stress and inconvenience of being confined during their season, every six months. They are also spared the physical and emotional trauma of phantom pregnancies, accidental matings, pyometra and ovarian cancer.

Spaying does not make a bitch fat or lazy. Regular exercise and a controlled diet will keep her fit and slim. A bitch's coat can occasionally become slightly fluffier, and incontinence can sometimes be a problem in juvenile (early) spays.

WHEN TO SPAY?

Medical research suggests that spaying your bitch – as young as possible – significantly reduces the chances of mammary tumours in later life (see above). On this basis, some veterinary surgeons recommend spaying juveniles at around six months of age.

However, many vets and people who work with dogs believe that there may be some physical and emotional benefits in allowing a bitch to have at least one season before being spayed. Unlike male dogs, bitches appear to benefit hugely from going through puberty, as they seem to calm down and become emotionally mature after their first season. Guide Dogs for the Blind allows its working bitches to have a season before spaying them, as do London's Metropolitan Police Dog School and other working homes.

The dogs that can benefit most from having their first season are those which are excitable and obviously immature, destructive or persistently pushy and domineering with either people or other dogs. This tactic also works well where the bitch has toilet training problems.

Left Carefully consider all the factors before deciding at what age to spay your bitch.

to be midway between seasons. If one assumes a six-month cycle, the right time should be three calendar months after the end of the season, when all of your bitch's hormones should have returned to their normal levels.

Above Your bitch need not become fat after spaying, but always keep a check on her weight in any case.

particularly incontinence, or suffers from submissive or excitable urination.

If your bitch is a paragon of virtue and doesn't exhibit any of the symptoms listed above, it's probably alright to spay her as a juvenile, before her first season arrives.

However, if she does have any of these symptoms, allowing her one season before spaying is likely to prove beneficial, both physically and mentally.

The most important thing is not to spay during any hormonal activity, so try to avoid spaying around the time you would expect your bitch to come into or be in season, or during a phantom pregnancy. The best time to spay appears

PAWS FOR THOUGHT

There is no truth in the old wive's tale that allowing your bitch to have a litter is beneficial. On the contrary, having a litter can serve to make her bossy and matriarchal, which is not always a good thing. It can also be very risky for the bitch, and you would be very upset if anything bad happened to your pet.

Good dog breeding takes considerable knowledge and experience, and the responsibilities (and potential costs) are enormous. This is undoubtedly something best left to the experts.

There is also the moral argument. There are more dogs in this world than there are good homes. The rescue centres are constantly bulging at the seams with surplus dogs, and thousands of dogs are destroyed every year because there aren't enough good homes to go round. Is there really a need for yet another litter of puppies, simply for the sake of it?

8 A DOG'S DINNER

A good, balanced diet is the sure way to keep your dog healthy and happy. Just as with humans, inner health equals outer beauty, and the first step to ensuring that your four-legged friend always looks and feels its best is to make sure that you provide it with all the nutrients, vitamins and minerals it requires. Most adult dogs should be fed twice a day, although some individuals are greedy and would like to receive more – but however wolfish your dog's appetite, be disciplined and ration your dog's food according to its needs, not its wants.

DELICIOUS AND DRY, OR TASTY AND TINNED?

Dog food manufacturers have invested huge sums of money in researching the nutritional requirements of dogs and making sure that they are all included in dry and canned food, both of which will give your hound a healthy diet.

All that gravy, jelly and meaty chunks may almost tempt you to add a sprig of parsley before serving some canned food, however, dry food is undoubtedly more convenient to use and results in compact

Right Puppies should be fed a special growth food, but resist the temptation to overfeed.

stools, which are easier to clean up. Bear in mind, though, that a dog fed on dry food requires more water to drink than one that is fed on canned food.

The thought of eating the same meal every night may fill us with horror, but there's no proof that boredom with food plays any part in a dog's appetite. The key is to find a dog food that is palatable and nutritious, and stick with it.

WHAT'S FOR DINNER?

There are many different feeding regimes to choose from: dry complete diets, canned food and biscuit mixer, cooked home-made food, and a raw 'natural' diet. Whatever your choice, it is important to understand that the quality of the food varies enormously within each diet and also between manufacturers.

DRY 'COMPLETE' FOODS

The cheapest (and lowest quality) dry complete foods often have

a high grain content (almost like muesli) and increase nutritional content by adding soya as a cheap source of protein. This diet does not suit all dogs, as many are sensitive or intolerant to grains – particularly wheat and soya products.

Premium-quality foods have correspondingly better quality ingredients. Most are based on chicken and corn (maize), which suits most dogs really well. Although at first glance these foods can appear too expensive, they are more digestible than lower grade foods, so that you don't need to feed such large amounts to your dog. In fact, many of them actually work out to be the same cost in total outlay, if not cheaper.

If a chicken and corn formula does not suit your dog (see page 102 for signs of food intolerance), try a lamb and rice formula. This has proven very successful for dogs with sensitive digestive systems. Just make sure that you are not confusing the issue by giving additional treats with 'suspect' ingredients – all treats must complement your dog's diet.

If your dog cannot tolerate lamb and rice, there are other special exclusion diets you can try – fish and potato, turkey and rice, fish and corn, duck and rice, fish and tapioca, and so on. Your vet will be able to advise you about what foods to experiment with until you find the right combination.

CANNED FOOD AND BISCUIT MIXER

Again, these vary in quality from brand to brand, so always check the label to see exactly what's in the can.

Some canned dog foods require a complementary biscuit mixer, which is not a good option for dogs with a wheat intolerance. Also, sometimes the biscuits themselves contain artificial colouring, which can present its own problems. However, some canned foods are rehydrated versions of the premium dry foods and do not require biscuits to 'balance' them – these can be a better choice for some dogs.

COOKED HOME-MADE FOOD

Unless you are an experienced canine nutritionist – and, let's face it, it can be difficult enough to keep an eye on your own diet – it is unlikely that you will feed your dog a home-made diet that is sufficiently balanced. Nutritional supplements may help, but oversupplementing can be as harmful to a dog as undersupplementing. Always consult your vet before starting down this road.

Left Keep your dog's food and water bowls clean and germ-free.

THE BONES AND RAW FOOD DIET

Essentially, some people believe that highly processed food is unsuitable for dogs and that a diet consisting of raw, meaty bones and fresh vegetables is a far healthier alternative. The bones and raw food diet needs proper planning and should not be undertaken without a great deal of research and understanding. It is certainly not the easy option. There are books available on the subject, and information about this diet can also be found on the Internet.

This approach is not without its problems, including the obvious one of achieving a correct balance of nutrients in the right amounts. Finding

Right Older dogs should benefit from a special geriatric diet.

a good source of healthy raw meat and bones is imperative – dogs, too, are susceptible to salmonella and campylobacter food poisoning. Another potential problem is the pesticide residues on fresh vegetables, so only organic vegetables bought from reputable grocers and suppliers should be used. On top of this, there is the worry of bone shards damaging your dog's gut.

The main advocates of the bones and raw food diet appear to be people whose dogs have dietary intolerances and who have found this approach beneficial. It may be worth considering if the premium-quality dry exclusion diets have not met your dog's needs.

FOOD SENSITIVITIES AND INTOLERANCES

There is anecdotal evidence suggesting that some dogs are sensitive or intolerant to certain ingredients and additives, and that these can cause a variety of problems.

Common symptoms include: general malaise (which can lead to hyperactive or aggressive behaviour), chronic skin and ear problems (for no apparent reason), light to mid-brown loose and bulky stools or diarrhoea, slime and jelly being passed with the stools and flatulence, bloating and weight gain.

In extreme cases, these dogs can suffer from colitis (slime and blood in their stools). Consult your vet if you notice any of the symptoms listed above.

The most common food intolerances are to artificial colourings, sugars, wheat, milk and soya. One of my clients is a 'leading world authority' on food allergies and intolerances, and he confirmed that the same holds true in humans. Obviously not all dogs are sensitive to these things, however, if the symptoms sound familiar, there may be some benefit in avoiding these ingredients for a couple of months

Right Be careful about what treats you give your dog, as some of them are unhealthy, at the very least.

to see if this has any beneficial effect on your dog's behaviour.

To pinpoint a possible food intolerance, avoid giving your dog any foods or treats containing the ingredients above for eight weeks, then reintroduce each item one at a time, watching for the return of any physical or behavioural changes after each addition. The treats should complement the diet, so use some of your dog's dinner (from its daily allowance) as treats.

TITBIT

Most commercial treats are highly processed and contain lots of sugar, artificial colourings, dairy products and fat. Even 'doggy chocs' or 'low-fat yogurt drops' contain sugars or lactose (milk sugar), so always read the label before you buy them. Avoid giving your dog any

PAWS FOR THOUGHT

Real chocolate is poison to dogs. It can cause liver damage and, in some cases, prove fatal. You must never give your dog chocolate or leave any lying around for it to find and eat. Be especially careful around holidays and birthdays. If the worst has happened and your dog has eaten chocolate, take it to the vet's surgery without delay.

sweet biscuits or sugary treats. These are bad for its teeth as well as its waistline, and they can cause sugar 'highs' and 'lows'. It is far better to stick to dried fish and meat pieces. Dried tripe stick and desiccated liver tablets often prove much more popular with your hound than boring pieces of doggie biscuit.

Collect and freeze a variety of table scraps for a reliable source of healthy, tasty treats, but remember to defrost them before offering them to your dog. Most dogs would sell their soul for a tasty scrap of cooked chicken or fish. Small pieces of vegetable and fruit can also be popular with dogs, but always peel them or use organic produce to avoid feeding your dog pesticide residues along with the treat.

FEEDING TIPS

🐾 Dogs should always be fed at regular times – any food left after 15 minutes of being put down should be removed and thrown away. If you leave food down, your dog will think it can eat when it likes, rather than at mealtimes. This regimen is particularly important with puppies, as it will help them with house training.

🐾 Eight-week-old puppies should be fed four times a day. Gradually increase the amount of food as your puppy grows, and switch to three meals a day when

Below Make sure that you control your dog's food intake carefully.

it is four months old or if it loses interest in one of the meals.

🐾 Change to two meals a day when your puppy is six months old, and keep it on two meals a day for the rest of its life. It is easier on your dog's digestive system to be fed two smaller meals rather than one large meal each day. This is especially important for medium to large breeds, which are more prone to gastric torsion, or bloat. This also gives your dog two meals to look forward to and keeps its energy levels on more of an even keel.

🐾 Never make any abrupt changes to your dog's diet. If you do alter its diet, spread the change over several days, gradually decreasing the old food and increasing the new. If you have any trouble getting your dog to eat its new diet, try pouring some warm water over its dinner. Don't be tempted to use stock cubes, as these are usually high in salt and monosodium glutamate.

🐾 Dogs can have quite sensitive digestive systems, so it is better to feed only one type (and flavour) of food to them. Don't use supplements unless they are recommended by your vet, as these can do more harm than good.

🐾 Always give your dog access to fresh, clean drinking water. Never let it drink from puddles, streams or ponds, as the

Above Feeding from the table can turn your dog into a beggar.

water could be polluted or contaminated with parasites that could make it ill.

🐾 Don't allow your dog to beg for or demand food. Never feed it from the table or put the scrapings from your plate into its bowl. This associates the practice with your meal, which will teach the dog to expect it and to beg. If you must give your dog scraps, put them in the refrigerator and give them with its next meal or freeze them and use them as treats.

🐾 Once your dog has learnt its feeding times, it may try to hurry the proceedings with attention-seeking behaviour, such as barking or begging. Don't give in to this –

you will only regret it later. Wait until the dog has stopped misbehaving or acting up before feeding it.

🐾 Some owners think that their dogs are fussy because they don't eat all their food, when in fact they are simply being overfed. Many food manufacturers have overly generous feeding guidelines and most people can feed their dog between 20 percent and 50 percent less than the recommended amounts to maintain its ideal weight. Weigh your dog regularly to make sure that it stays at its optimum weight. If it hasn't eaten for a day or two, have it checked over by your vet to ensure that there is nothing wrong.

🐾 At the other of the spectrum, there are dogs that are greedy and appear to be perpetually starving (most commonly gun dogs). Many would simply eat until they were sick, then start all over again. If your dog has this kind of seemingly voracious appetite, you must ignore its appeals.

🐾 Your dog's stool quality should be consistently dark brown and firm. If stools start firm and become softer at the end, this is probably a sign of overfeeding. Reweigh the food, and compare it to the recommended amount. If necessary, cut back the amount by 10 to 20 percent.

🐾 If the stools are not consistently dark brown and firm, or your dog is flatulent,

either the food does not suit it or it may be unwell. Check with your vet before doing anything else.

🐾 Antibiotics can upset a dog's digestive system (and stool quality) and should be followed with a course of probiotics to re-establish the 'friendly' gut bacteria that aid digestion. You can get probiotics from your vet or pet supply store. Don't give live yogurt, as most adult dogs can't digest milk properly, and it gives them wind and diarrhoea.

🐾 Never feed your dog before exercise or play, as running about on a full stomach can be very bad for dogs. It is far better to feed it at least an hour after any exercise and allow it a period of quiet for at least two hours after its meal.

Above Do not to confuse your dog's greed with hunger.

🐾 Don't feed your dog before a car journey, as this encourages car sickness. Make sure your dog has access to fresh water at the journey's end.

🐾 Medium to large breeds should be fed from a raised bowl to prevent them swallowing air and straining their necks while feeding. This also helps to prevent bloat or stomach torsion.

🐾 Don't take your dog's food bowl away from it while it is eating. This will only make it anxious about your presence near its bowl and is one of the most common causes of food aggression. Instead, leave it to eat its meal in peace.

AVOIDING BLOAT

Gastric, or stomach, dilation and torsion, commonly known as 'bloat', is a canine medical emergency requiring immediate veterinary attention. If the stomach contents (food and gases) cannot escape because the gut is blocked or twisted, the stomach can rapidly swell up like a balloon, crushing and damaging the vital organs. This can rapidly degenerate into a fatal situation.

Most dogs show obvious signs of pain and discomfort. They will become restless and find it difficult to settle (some owners think their dogs are being naughty). Some dogs stretch the front of the body in what looks like a 'play bow' or arch their back. Some will try to vomit, but are not always able to do so. The dog may salivate profusely, and the stomach feels tight like a drum skin when tapped. Breathing becomes more difficult. The dog may then go into shock, collapse, fall into unconsciousness and die. The onset of 'bloat' can be very rapid, so it is vital that you get your dog to the veterinary surgeon without delay.

Bloat often occurs between 9 pm and midnight, as dogs are often fed in the evening, then (wrongly) taken for a walk before the stomach is completely empty. However, it can strike at any time so don't assume that it will always fall into this timetable.

A dog of any size can suffer this affliction, although it is more common in large dogs with a deep chest – German shepherds, boxers, retrievers and Great Danes, for example. It is essential that you learn how to recognize the symptoms of bloat, what to do if it happens and how to minimize the risks.

Left Owners of medium-sized and large dogs should keep a wary eye out for any signs of bloat.

PAWS FOR THOUGHT

There are several precautions you should take in order to minimize the risks of bloat:

● Do not allow your dog to run around or play on a full stomach, otherwise there is a danger that the stomach could swing out of place and twist the gut. Be aware of this for several hours after each meal.

● Overloading the stomach increases the likelihood of bloat. Choose a dry complete food that is concentrated (so that you can feed lesser amounts) and highly digestible (so that it doesn't remain in the stomach for longer than necessary). Control your dog's food intake, and never allow it to have free access to unlimited food. Do not feed a dry food that expands excessively when soaked, unless you pre-soak it before feeding. Divide your dog's daily ration into two smaller meals, rather than giving one large meal.

● Reduce the potential for air to enter the stomach. Feed your dog from a raised bowl to reduce air intake, and do not feed or water your dog when it is panting. Avoid foods that cause burping and flatulence, such as milk, a common cause of wind in adult dogs.

9 GOOD GROOMING

To keep your dog in the peak of health – not to mention being the most gorgeous specimen in the neighbourhood – you need to know how to care properly for it. Nails, teeth, coat and ears all need regular checking and attention, and your dog needs to become accustomed to being bathed, groomed and checked all over. This chapter tells you what you need to know and how to implement it.

THE BENEFITS OF BRUSHING

Short-coated dogs, such as Labradors, should be groomed regularly, as they can moult copiously and their short, spiky hair can be a scourge on clothes, furnishings and carpets. Use a short bristle or rubber-toothed brush which will massage and stimulate the dog's skin, increase the circulation and work out any loose hair. A wipeover with a damp chamois leather will leave a nice shine.

Medium- and long-coated dogs should be groomed and detangled every day – just make certain that you use the right type of brush to suit your dog's coat. Detangling is often easiest with a human's hairbrush with thick white nylon teeth or a comb with revolving teeth. The undercoat can

then be brushed out, but be careful not to scratch your dog's skin if you are using a wire brush. Don't drag your brush through knotted fur. Instead, cut the knots out with round-ended scissors.

Some long-coated dogs, such as spaniels, become really tangled and knotty behind the ears, in the armpits, between the toes and on the backs of the thighs. These areas are easier to manage if you keep the hair trimmed short and groom your dog regularly.

Certain breeds need to have their coat clipped or hand-stripped regularly. You can learn to do this yourself or have a groomer do it for you.

Most people brush their dogs far too vigorously, which overexcites them and makes them jumpy. Brush your dog slowly and gently, with the same care you would expect from your hairdresser.

At first, allow your dog to become used to being stroked all over, then gently and slowly brush its coat with a soft brush. If it tries to bite the brush,

anoint the edges with a little clove oil – it tastes disgusting. This will convince the dog not to bother resisting and is a better option than pulling the brush away when it snaps.

Left and right Whether your dog is a low-maintenance mutt or a high-maintenance madam, regular grooming is essential.

HEALTH CHECK

Grooming your dog regularly not only keeps its coat and skin in prime condition, but also gives you the opportunity to check all over its body for any lumps, swellings, rashes, cuts, grass seeds and such like. Also check your dog's teeth, gums, nails (especially its dew claws – see page 110), eyes and ears regularly.

1 TEACH YOUR DOG TO STAND STILL AND TOLERATE BEING HANDLED AND EXAMINED. This will also help to prepare your dog for visits to the veterinary surgeon

Right Distract and reward your dog while you are examining it.

(see page 69 for tips on training your dog to stand still for examination).

2 HOLD A FEW TREATS IN FRONT OF THE DOG'S NOSE WITH ONE HAND. Meanwhile, run your other hand down its back to the tip of its tail. Next, starting with the front legs, run your hand down each leg, all the way down to the paws. Then do the same with the back legs.

3 REPEAT THE ENTIRE PROCESS, THIS TIME PICKING UP EACH PAW. Gently hold the paw in the palm of your hand a little way off the floor. Do not to pull the dog's paws into an uncomfortable position, throw it off balance or hurt it, or it will learn not to trust you. Be firm, but gentle and considerate. If your dog tries to kick its legs about or pull its paws away, follow the movement with your hand, but do not let go until it has relaxed and given in.

4 DISPENSE TREATS FREQUENTLY TO MAINTAIN THE DOG'S INTEREST IN YOUR OTHER HAND. If it tries to run off, put its lead on and tread or kneel on the lead, or tether it to keep both hands free.

5 IF YOUR DOG TRIES TO STRUGGLE AND SQUIRM, DO NOT WITHDRAW. Let your hands be limp and passive, stop talking and avoid eye contact – in other words, ignore the dog's objections. Wait until the dog tires and stops, then praise it and let it go. This reinforces the lesson that only good behaviour gets it off the hook.

6 DO NOT BEHAVE IN A THREATENING FASHION WHILE YOU HAVE YOUR DOG IN THIS VULNERABLE POSITION. Do not shout or become impatient with the dog; it must relax in order to tolerate handling.

7 YOUR DOG MUST BECOME USED TO BEING HANDLED AROUND ITS BOTTOM. It will otherwise be intolerant of having its temperature taken.

8 UNCASTRATED MALE DOGS NEED TO HAVE THEIR TESTICLES CHECKED. Look for changes that could indicate testicular cancer. Bitches need their chests and abdomen checked for mammary tumours. If you detect changes, consult your vet.

EYES

Let your dog become used to you running your fingers lightly around its eye area, so that you can wipe away any 'sleep' and check for grass seeds that may become lodged inside the eyelids.

EARS

Inspect and smell both ears regularly to check for any grass seeds or infection in the ear canal. Wipe away any dark brown wax with a tissue, but don't poke around with cotton buds, as you'll just push the wax further into the ear canal.

If your dog is producing a lot of brown wax, or if its ears smell bad, take it to the vet immediately. Ear infections can quickly become chronic and cause permanent damage. Other indications of an ear infection are the dog tilting its head, scratching its ears excessively or rubbing its ears against you, the carpet or the furnishings.

NAILS

Most dogs wear their nails down if they are walked on pavement or concrete regularly. However, if your dog only walks on grass or carpet, its nails may grow excessively long and cause discomfort. They will need regular trimming. Ask your vet or groomer to trim them or show you how to do it.

Trimming long nails can be difficult, as you have to avoid cutting or crushing the pink 'quick' area, which is the nerve and blood supply. If you damage this by accident, it will bleed and be painful, and your dog may never let you near its feet again. The 'quick' is easy to identify on white nails, but not on black ones. Ask the vet or groomer to do this if you're unsure.

DEW CLAWS

These are the little 'thumbs' on the inside of the dogs 'wrists'. Some dogs will have had them removed, while others may still have them on all four legs. Dew claws do not wear down like normal nails and grow in a circle. They can cut into the flesh if they grow too long, so check them regularly as they may need trimming.

ANAL GLANDS

Dogs have two small scent glands just inside their anus. Occasionally, these can become overfull, leading to infection and a substantial amount of pain. If your dog drags its bottom along the ground or whips round to nibble at the base of its tail, or even if it chases its tail, the anal glands may need emptying. You can learn how to do this yourself, or ask your vet or groomer to do it for you.

Right Excessive scratching should always be investigated to determine its cause.

TEETH

Puppies start losing their baby teeth at about four and a half months old and should have a full set of adult teeth by six months. Sadly, the majority of dogs have bad teeth and gums by the time they are three years old. Most of these will go on to have difficulty eating or playing with toys because of sore gums and toothache, and will lose their teeth prematurely. Bad teeth and gums cause chronic bad breath and allow bacteria to enter the bloodstream. Tooth decay is entirely preventable, so follow these tips:

Avoid giving your dog any sweet biscuits or sugary treats. Most commercial treats contain large amounts of sugar. Always check the label on store-bought products, and stick to meaty or fishy treats, or bits of fresh, preferably organic vegetable, such as carrot.

Give your dog special chew toys that help to clean its teeth, such as rigid nylon bones, nylon rope toys or tightly rolled rawhide chews. See page 118 for more information on these.

Brush your dog's teeth a couple of times a week. Prepare your dog first by getting it used to having its mouth and lips touched, then give it a (sugar-free) treat. Run a finger under its lips, and trace it around the gum line. It is not necessary to open the dog's mouth, but it will help to hold onto its collar while you are doing this. Take your time, and expect to make slow progress. Do not force the issue. Once the dog is familiar and comfortable with having its mouth touched, you can move on to using a special 'finger toothbrush' from your vet. These are very easy to use and far less alarming to your dog than an ordinary toothbrush.

You can also use an 'enzymatic' toothpaste especially designed for dogs to keep your pooch's teeth in tiptop condition. It is available from your vet and breaks down the plaque and controls bacteria. Either apply this paste directly onto the teeth or smear it on your dog's chew toys. Do not use 'human' toothpaste or baking soda, as both these can cause a variety of health problems.

You can ensure trips to the vets go smoothly. Most vets like to examine dogs (except the really big ones) on a table, so you should ensure your dog is unperturbed by being lifted on and off a table. It also needs to be accustomed to standing still while you hold its collar and gently support it under the tummy. This will be useful when the vet has to take its temperature – you certainly don't want your precious hound sitting down on the thermometer unexpectedly or jumping off the table.

While it is restrained like this, ask a member of the family to hold a treat right up to its nose as they run their hands along its body, legs, feet, ears and gums, so it becomes familiar and happy with this set-up. Use a non-slip bath mat to protect your tabletop and to prevent your dog from slipping.

HYGIENE TIPS FOR THE ACTIVE CANINE

Dogs do not perspire as humans do, so they should not need bathing as often. In fact, frequent washing can remove the coat's protective oils and simply make it more likely to collect dirt. Unless your dog has rolled in something particularly disgusting, a bath every six months should do it, although there are exceptions:

Some male dogs have a tendency to urinate on their front legs or on their chest fur. If this happens, rinse it off after a walk and trim away any excess fur.

Swimming is not always the safest activity, as dogs can pick up all sorts of serious disorders from swimming or wading in stagnant or polluted water. Death is even possible in extreme cases, so make sure that you rinse off your dog immediately and bathe it properly as soon as possible. Prevention can be the best approach, as once dogs learn to enjoy swimming, it can be hard to keep them out of the water – and they will show no

Above It should only be necessary to bathe your dog every six months – unless it rolls in something smelly.

discernment between a crystal-clear stream and a stinking cesspool.

Some dogs love rolling in cow pats, horse dung or just about any kind of putrid matter that you can think of – to them, it is the ultimate perfume. In these cases, immediate bathing is justified. Resist reaching for highly scented shampoo, as this will only make your dog more likely to roll again at the first opportunity.

Tomato juice or ketchup neutralizes the lingering smell of fox faeces. Apply it, let it dry, then brush it out and shampoo your dog as usual.

If your dog has a decidedly doggy odour without an obvious explanation, such as bad teeth or a dirty coat, it could be that its food (particularly canned food) is making it smell – not a socially acceptable characteristic. Try a change of diet to see if this helps.

BATHING

If washing your dog in the bath, put down a rubber mat to prevent it slipping. If bathing your dog outside, tie it up and use a watering can of tepid water. Always dry your dog properly, especially around its joints. Gentle towelling and a cool or warm hairdryer work well, but try not to be too vigorous with the towelling or your dog will turn the whole process into a game.

TITBIT

When it comes to worming, flea and tick control, and vaccinations, your vet can advise you on what to use and how regularly. Put the dates in your diary or on a calendar in the kitchen, as not all vets send reminders.

Only use a hairdryer if your dog is used to it. Never use hot water or a hot hairdryer, as dogs cannot cope with it as we can, and make sure that you do not get water in your dog's ears.

Below and right Wash your dog's head and face last, or it may shake prematurely and drench you.

SHOP TILL YOU DROP

We've looked at the ideal exercise regime, instilling good manners and satisfying appetite; now here's the really important stuff – shopping. This is where you can indulge in your love for accessorizing – within reason – and kit your dog out with the latest canine essentials and not-so-essentials. From practical basics that your hound simply cannot do without to all those little things that will help your dog to stand out from the pack, there are a wealth of products and accessories. And these days you can find it all without having to sacrifice your sense of style.

THE ESSENTIALS
COLLARS

Nylon collars are the best option, as they are strong but gentle on your dog's neck, and do not stretch or rot. Buy one with a strong metal buckle fastener – avoid those with a plastic 'quick-release' clip, as these break more easily and can accidentally come undone if you try to hold your dog by its collar.

Leather collars and leads can become dry and brittle unless they are looked after properly, meaning that they may break suddenly – and it is all too likely that this will be at a crucial moment when control is all-important. They also have a tendency to stretch and can easily become dangerously loose. If you do choose a leather collar, you must check its size and condition regularly.

Metal collars (such as check chains) can damage your dog's coat and pinch and injure its neck – and you certainly don't want to choke your faithful friend. As metal collars are slipped on over the head, they can obviously also slip off, making them less secure than a buckled collar. There are some breeds of dog,

Left and right Nylon equipment is stronger and easier to look after than leather, but can look cheap.

such as rough collies and Shetland sheepdogs, that have a thicker neck than head. If your dog falls into this category, it might be more secure on a check chain or half-check collar, which tightens when the dog pulls backwards.

Left Check chains are unnecessary and can damage your dog's coat and neck.

TITBIT

Your dog's collar should be comfortably loose – you should be able to fit two fingers under it without strangling your dog – but tight enough that it can't slide over your dog's head if the dog pulls backwards. If you can pull the collar to the top of the dog's neck and work the collar over one ear, it is too loose.

LEADS

Nylon and chain leads can cut into and hurt your hands, so you may be better off with a rope lead. But if your dog likes to chew or bite at its lead, then a chain lead is probably the better choice.

Extending leads encourage dogs to pull and can be dangerous to use near roads – imagine if your dog were to run out into the road and the lead were not locked in time. Furthermore, extending leads should not be used in the park.

They can ensnare and injure other dogs and people, and they are often too short to be of any real use. A trailing long line (a 20–40 metre (60–120 feet) piece of strong cord with a dog clip on the end) is generally a safer option and a more useful length (see page 49).

Above

There is a huge range of products to choose from, even when it comes to basic items such as leads and collars, and these days you can combine fashion with practicality.

IDENTITY DISCS

When it comes to identity discs, the engraved metal ones are best, as the barrel types often come apart and lose their information.

Ensure that the identity disc attaches to your dog's collar with a good-quality split ring. If not, use one from an old key ring. A word of warning: always attach the lead to the 'D' ring on the collar and not the split ring (a common mistake), as it isn't strong enough to take your dog's weight.

MICROCHIPPING

Having your dog microchipped is a more permanent method of identification and one that will give you greater peace of mind. Microchipping means that, if the worst happened and your dog were lost (and found) without its collar and identity disc, the microchip could be 'scanned' and your dog quickly and easily identified. Most vets offer this service.

POOP SCOOP BAGS

You are legally obliged to pick up and dispose of your dog's faeces in most places now, so always carry plastic 'poo bags' with you whenever you take your dog out. Even if it is not compulsory, it is certainly the socially and environmentally correct thing to do. Always carry a spare bag to offer (and embarrass) any less responsible dog owners.

Poop scoop bags can be bought at most veterinary surgeries, pet stores and dog training clubs, or you can use nappy bags or food bags. Don't, whatever you do, use carrier bags with holes in them. Keep the bags by the front door, so that they are readily to hand when you are on the way out for a walk.

Use the bag like a glove, pick up the faeces, invert the bag (like pulling off a rubber glove), knot it and dispose of it properly – that is, in a litter bin or your garbage can at home. If you recoil at the mere thought of picking it up like this, it is possible to buy special plastic jaws to use instead of your hand – but these can be awkward to carry and a little conspicuous.

BEDDING

Don't buy an expensive dog bed until your puppy is fully grown and has finished teething. Until then, use a large cardboard box or plastic oval dog bed big enough for the dog to stretch out in when fully grown, as not all dogs like sleeping curled up.

Don't buy a wicker basket, as dogs love chewing them and wicker can prove dangerously sharp. Bear in mind that dogs also love chewing beanbags – a cleaning catastrophe simply waiting to happen if ever there was one.

Once your dog is all grown up and less likely to chew, a nice foam bed or folded fibre duvet or comforter makes an

Below Even designers such as Bill Amberg have moved into offering stylish accoutrements for pets.

excellent bed. Don't use a feather duvet or comforter, as it is likely to be chewed and more difficult to wash. If you want to line your dog's bed, use towels or duvet covers, rather than blankets. The latter are harder to keep clean and more likely to develop that distinctive 'doggie' smell.

Large or heavy breeds of dog need a bed with a deep foam mattress so that they do not develop pressure sores.

BRUSHES AND COMBS

Good grooming is important to the well-heeled dog. There are many different types of brushes and combs available (see page 108 for ideas), and you may like to ask your breeder or grooming parlour for advice on what to buy.

TREATS

Commercially available treats tend to be full of artificial colourings, sugars and fats. Try to buy more natural treats – dried liver, dried tripe sticks (cut into small pieces) and dried fish, for example. Alternatively, make your own tasty treats by saving and freezing table scraps.

Right Most dogs love a Kong stuffed with food, and they can provide almost endless enjoyment.

TOYS

It is very important that your dog has appropriate toys to play with. This should encourage it to play with its own toys – and not yours or your children's.

Toys provide mental stimulation and can divert your dog away from chewing other articles   such as your favourite Italian shoes – something which is especially important during a puppy's 'teething' phase. Chew toys also keep your dog's teeth clean and

Right Buy your dog a variety of toys that you can bait with food.

TITBIT
Don't allow your dog to take its toys into the garden or backyard. It will only bury them and you may never see them again. Keep most toys up off the floor in a toybox so that you can offer them in rotation. This should make them more desirable; otherwise, just as with children, your dog can become fed up with seeing the same toys every day. Just remember to ensure that there is always something out for it to find and play with.

allow it to exercise its jaws, helping to burn off excess energy.

If you are experiencing the joys of living in a multi-dog household, bear in mind that it pays to tie similar toys in different parts of the room to prevent any squabbling. Dogs, like toddlers, can have difficulty grasping the concept of sharing.

PLASTIC BONES

Specially designed rigid nylon bones (not the bendy ones) and toys are quite good for cleaning your dog's teeth, but make sure that it cannot chew or bite small chunks off and swallow them, as this is a potential choking hazard.

ROPE TOYS AND TUGGIES

Nylon fibre rope tuggies are hygienic and good for flossing teeth and massaging gums. You can insert dry

Above Nylon and cotton rope toys allow a dog to play tug-of-war, chew, shred and shake.

PAWS FOR THOUGHT

There is no doubt that a dog and its bone are not so easily parted, but this doesn't necessarily make them a good idea. Raw or cooked meaty bones that are left down can harbour germs and cause food poisoning. Dogs are also extremely likely to hide them as they are so valued, so don't give them to your dog. Don't give the cooked bones of pork, lamb, chicken or beef, as these can crumble or splinter and injure your dog. The only type of cooked bone that is acceptable is a strong sterilized or smoked marrow bone with the marrow and all the meat removed. You can make sterilized bones more interesting by stuffing some food down the middle, as long as you regularly scrub them out and pour boiling water over them to re-sterilize them. Excessive chewing on bones can wear down or break your dog's tooth enamel, so check its teeth regularly for damage.

treats into the coils of the fibres to gain and maintain the dog's attention. Do not leave your dog alone with cotton rope toys, as they are easy to shred and your dog could swallow and choke on the loose threads. Also, the cotton absorbs saliva and can become laden with bacteria, so wash your dog's cotton toys in boiling water regularly.

CHEW TOYS

Tightly rolled rawhide chews are popular and are said to be beneficial for tooth cleaning, however, they are only safe if your dog chews them, rather than swallowing big pieces. Take the rawhide chew away when it becomes either small enough to swallow or when you are not there to watch over your dog. You don't want the dog to pull off a strip and choke on it.

Don't give your dog coloured rawhide chews. These can stain carpets and furnishings, and some dogs react adversely to the artificial colourings.

Below Toys that bounce unpredictably are great fun.

TOP TOY TIPS

● Don't give squeaky toys to your dog – especially a terrier – or it may learn to associate high-pitched noises with the killing game. You don't want your dog to confuse this with children, who can make similar sounds. Apart from this, the noise can be very irritating.

● Don't let your dog play with new tennis balls in case it shreds off the felt and swallows it. Only old, bald tennis balls are suitable and only then as long as your dog cannot get one stuck in its mouth or throat.

● Never allow your dog to play with squash balls or golf balls. It could swallow these with lethal results. Larger balls on ropes are much safer.

● Never throw sticks for your dog or allow it to chew them. It could impale itself on them or be poked in the eye while catching or carrying them. Splinters could also become embedded in its mouth, throat or stomach, causing abscesses – or worse – needing veterinary attention. If you want to play 'catch' or 'fetch', use a nylon Frisbee or a large ball or Kong on a rope. These come in different sizes, are easy to clean and carry, and are much safer.

INTERESTING TOYS

Some toys are designed to be stuffed with food or to bounce around unpredictably. These provide hours of fun either on their own or in play with you. You can buy Kongs or activity balls or cubes from good pet stores or over the Internet, but you need to make absolutely certain that your dog cannot destroy the toy before you the two are left alone together.

A large ball (or Kong) on a rope is very good for playing fetch, as it prevents the dog from accidentally swallowing the ball and is a lot easier to keep a firm hold on if your dog decides to play tug-of-war. Don't leave your dog alone with this toy, otherwise it could chew off the rope. Only use it during walks or play sessions.

CAR HARNESSES

Car harnesses can be a very useful item, so find one that is adjustable and that has

padding around the chest area for extra comfort and safety.

BOWLS TO DROOL OVER

With the vast choice of designs and sizes available, your canine companion can always dine in style.

Most importantly, choose a bowl that your dog won't be able to tip over easily – or buy a rack to hold it upright. A heavy ceramic bowl is ideal if your dog likes to push it around or play with it.

Long-eared dogs, such as spaniels, are best fed from bowls that have a small opening. Their ears will fall outside the bowl and not trail in their food and water.

Medium and large breeds should be fed from a bowl raised to their shoulder height to prevent stomach torsion or bloat (see page 105). You can buy special bowl stands and bowls at good pet stores or find them advertised in dog magazines.

Easy-to-clean solid stainless steel or glazed ceramic bowls are the ideal choice. Some earthenware and plastic bowls are porous and collect microscopic particles of food making them nearly impossible to keep clean. Plastic bowls are also tempting

Left Car harnesses are very useful, but you should never let your dog hang out of an open window.

Above Your dog should have its own food and water bowl

to chew. Place the dog's bowl on a wipe-clean rubber or plastic mat to keep food off the floor and make cleaning easier.

OPTIONAL EXTRAS
ANTI-PULLING TRAINING AIDS

There are lots of devices on the market that claim to help control or correct pulling on the lead. These range from a variety of head collars and harnesses aimed at controlling the dog gently, through to more severe collars, such as check chains and pronged 'pinch' collars.

Most people advocate the less severe approach and embrace the concept of head collars or anti-pull harnesses. Some designs are better than others, and the best ones can be very useful if you have a dog that is too strong for you.

HEAD COLLARS

Models with adjustable cheek-straps
and a cushioned noseband ensure a
comfortable fit. Other designs can tend
to squeeze your dog's face uncomfortably
and ride up into the dog's eyes. Most dogs,
understandably, don't like this at all.

If you are using a head collar, your dog
should always wear another collar and
lead as a back-up in case the head collar
slips off or its plastic clip breaks.
Alternatively, you could use a half- or full-
check chain as your back-up collar. The
extra play of the free end of the chain
collar would enable you to use just one
lead attached to both.

HARNESSES

Harnesses are generally unnecessary and
should not really be used with growing
dogs. However, dogs with neck or back
injuries and some breeds, such as English
bulldogs and Yorkshire terriers, can have
weak throats. These dogs may be better
off if walked on a harness.

For dogs that throw their weight into a
harness and pull even harder, there are
special anti-pulling harnesses which
squeeze the dog under the armpits when
it pulls. The best ones have extra padding
to protect this delicate area, but even so,
check that it is not rubbing the skin.

MUZZLE

If you need to muzzle your dog because it
scavenges or bites, choose one that allows
the dog to open its mouth, in case it needs
to pant, drink or vomit.

Wire 'cage' muzzles, such as those
worn by racing greyhounds, seem to be
secure and well tolerated, and come in
wide variety of sizes. You can probably
find out where to get one through your
local greyhound track, and these muzzles
can often be made to size.

'Wind sock' type muzzles commonly
sold in pet supply stores are unsuitable for
use during exercise. Some plastic basket
muzzles can be easily pulled off, but will
hurt your dog if attached too tightly. If you
use one, check for comfort and security.

INDOOR BARKITECTURE

Many owners find indoor kennels (dog
crates), play pens and child gates very
useful for controlling their puppy's
environment. This helps greatly with toilet
training and can keep the puppy away
from hazards, such as toddlers, stairs,
wires they can chew, carpets they can
urinate on, and all the normal household
detritus that they can swallow.

Dogs usually love having their own
den or 'four-poster bed' where they can
escape marauding children (and adults) –
just make sure that your dog is never
disturbed when it is in there.

OUTSIDE KENNELS AND DOG RUNS

If yours is an indoor dog used to shade
and central heating, don't leave it outside
in the sun or cold for any length of time.
Left to their own devices, these dogs will
wreck gardens, annoy neighbours and
become frustrated and wild.

If, on the other hand, your
dog loves the great outdoors
and hardly spends time inside,
it needs a proper kennel and run.
Seek specialist help designing
and building one.

Left Some dogs simply thrive on
having their own special 'house'.

STEPPING OUT IN STYLE

Every dog lover knows that their precious pooch deserves to be kept cosy in cold or wet weather. But rather like when you go to the gym, your furry friend needs to look the part for walkies in the park – no pooch wants to be the barking stock of other mutts, after all. The most practical coats are weather resistant with a snug lining, but there's a huge choice for style-conscious canines. These days, the best-dressed dogs wear cashmere, trouser suits and raincoats!

Right Clothing should serve a practical purpose and must also fit comfortably and securely, allowing the dog to move freely.

Some thin-skinned breeds with a low body fat ratio (such as whippets and Italian greyhounds) or recently clipped dogs really do feel the cold and shiver pathetically. These dogs, in particular, may benefit from wearing a special jumper or warm coat when out on walks. Dogs with very long coats and lots of feathering on their legs can also benefit from protective clothing, as it not only keeps them dry, but also free of mud. It may be worth trying out some different designs – and always try before you buy.

Although you can choose from a variety of designer makes, your dog's wellbeing should always come first – sacrificing comfort for style is not advisable, no matter how adorable you think your devoted friend looks. Make sure that the coat is well balanced and secure, and that the fastenings are not too tight and do not rub, particularly in areas where the skin is delicate. Also, don't forget to ensure that your dog can still perform its toilet duties, as some dogs will go on strike if they feel ill at ease.

Some dogs tolerate or learn to accept clothing, while others absolutely hate it and refuse to budge. Respect your dog's feelings and don't force the issue if your dog is unhappy.

Accessories, such as hats and boots, are unnecessary and impractical, and most dogs will not tolerate wearing them during exercise.

Clothing should be practical and designed for outside use. Don't keep your dog's clothes on when it is indoors or it will become overheated.

TITBIT

Don't forget who the coat is actually for. Take your dog with you on your shopping spree to check the fit of its new jacket. If your dog is likely to show you up and throw a tantrum, measure it in a straight line from the base of the tail to its neck, and leave it at home with its favourite toy.

AVOIDING BAD BEHAVIOUR

Most behaviour problems with dogs are entirely predictable. Very often the fault lies with the owners, whether they are simply allowing bad habits to grow through lack of understanding or corrupting their precious pets with kindness. All dogs need to be properly socialized as puppies, exercised properly, trained appropriately, groomed regularly and taught how to play appropriate games. They need to have the right kind of diet and toys, and to be taught that undesirable behaviour is unacceptable. If any of these areas are neglected, your dog is likely to develop training or behaviour problems, turning your pride and joy into the kind of mutt that gives the canine species a bad name. So here's what can go wrong and why, as well as some useful remedial tips.

WHEN YOUR DOG TURNS INTO A SCAREDY CAT

Socialize your dog properly so that it becomes familiar with what to expect when dealing with people, other dogs, children, traffic noises, travelling, and so on. Failure to do this causes fearful and aggressive behaviour.

MAKING A MESS

When it comes to toilet training, puppies need a steady, reliable routine. As already mentioned, regular input leads to regular output, so don't leave your puppy's food down for more than 15 minutes. Take your dog into the garden or backyard at regular intervals, and don't make the common

mistake of leaving the back door open or expecting the puppy to ask to go out when it needs to. See page 36 for more tips on successful toilet training.

BITING THE HAND THAT FEEDS IT

Don't take your dog's food away while it is eating. This is a common cause of food aggression. It is better to give your dog a small portion of its meal, then offer it more. This way, you will be seen as an asset to have around, rather than a threat. Remember, those primal hunting instincts are really not buried so deep – just think of men and barbecues.

BENEVOLENT DICTATORSHIP

Inappropriate correction can be the cause of aggression. Don't smack or shout at your dog; don't threaten it with a rolled-up newspaper or a rattle can; don't wag your finger in its face. Your dog will think that you are a bully, and it could well start answering you back in kind. It may even redirect its frustration and aggression onto

Left Early socialization with other dogs, people, children and traffic is essential to raising a happy and well-balanced dog.

someone else. Alternatively, it will wait until you are conspicuously absent before being naughty. Dogs can be devious, too. See page 47 for advice on how to correct appropriately and effectively.

BOISTEROUS BEHAVIOUR

Don't shut your dog out when it is being naughty. Out of sight will definitely end up being out of mind. If the dog becomes overly boisterous, ignore it, or deal with the behaviour effectively (see pages 52–3). Alternatively, tether the dog in the corner of the room (with a chew toy) until it calms down, then free it. In this way, your hound will soon learn that bad behaviour means restraint, and good behaviour lets it off the hook – literally.

BEING THE CENTRE OF ATTENTION

Don't automatically give your dog attention whenever it demands it. Once your dog thinks you are at its beck and call, it will expect your undivided attention – and annoy you until you succumb – wherever and whenever it wants.

Instead, occasionally ignore the dog for a few minutes. Only when it has given up trying to manipulate should you give it something constructive to do, such as a sit, down or recall. Then – and only then –

can you reward and fuss over it. By using your attention in a constructive way, you will be teaching your dog to be more responsive and respectful.

GRUMPY BEHAVIOUR

Your dog is not the only animal that needs to be taught proper attitudes. Teach your family and friends to respect your dog and its boundaries. Don't disturb the dog when it is lying down, resting or sleeping, because many children (and adults) are bitten by irritated dogs who just want to be left alone. Everyone, even canines, feels a little 'Marlena Dietrich' at times. Most dogs don't like being kissed, cuddled or hugged; this is the dog equivalent of having your cheek pinched and often makes dogs snappy towards faces. Hence, it is especially important to bear this in mind if you have children. See page 38 for a list of rules for dealing with the combination of children and dogs.

DOGGIE DEPENDENCE

Separation anxiety can become a real problem with some dogs if you don't endeavour to prevent it. While you certainly shouldn't be keeping a dog if you are never there to provide company, it is also true that you cannot possibly be with it 24 hours a day. Don't let your

Above Always let sleeping dogs lie. In fact, you should always let dogs that are awake, but enjoying a quiet moment, lie too.

dog become clingy and too dependent on your company. It will only become distressed when it is left alone, and you will not be able to leave it for even short periods of time (see page 54).

FEELING STIR CRAZY

Give your dog regular off-lead exercise where it can safely run free and socialize with other dogs. Dogs that do not receive enough exercise or mix with other dogs regularly become frustrated and are more prone to developing behaviour and training problems (see pages 82–9).

TOUCH SENSITIVE

Groom and handle your dog regularly. If you don't do this, you will have difficulty with grooming in general and more especially when your dog needs to be examined by a vet (see pages 106–13).

BEGGING FOR FOOD

Don't give your dog food from your plate, and don't scrape scraps from the plate into the dog's bowl. It will grow to expect it and start loitering and begging – with accompanying barking and drooling. Freeze any tasty leftovers and use them later (defrosted) as training rewards, or put them in the refrigerator and simply add them to its next meal.

SCAVENGING

Never drop treats to the floor for your dog or allow your dog to clean up dropped food. Only walk your dog in areas that are clear of rubbish and food wrappers. This is very important, as otherwise your dog will become a scavenger – a bad trait and one you don't want to encourage.

DISOBEDIENCE AND BAD MANNERS

A trained dog is easy to manage and a pleasure to own. Teach your dog to sit when being greeted (so it never jumps up) and to come back to you when called (so you can exercise it properly).

GARDEN DESTROYER

Dogs should not be put out or left on their own in your garden or backyard for any length of time.

Left Get your dog used to being left on its own so it doesn't mope whenever you are out.

They will quickly become bored and frustrated, making them territorial, noisy and destructive. They dig up the lawns and flowerbeds, bury their toys, destroy everything they can get hold of, bark at every little noise (aggravating the neighbours), learn to chase cats, squirrels and birds (which can develop into chasing joggers and cyclists in the park), eat bees and wasps (which can be very dangerous) and dive bomb visitors to 'their' garden.

Leaving the back door open so that they can come and go as they please can adversely affect their toilet training and recall response. Also, they will often bring bits of the garden back inside, so avoid this practice if you can.

GUARDING TERRITORY

Don't allow your dog routinely to sleep on your lap, bed or any of the furniture. This can easily progress to it guarding these areas from you or other members of the family. Make sure that it has a comfortable bed of its own, and encourage it to use that instead.

DIETARY DISORDERS

Feed your dog the best-quality diet that you can, especially while it is growing – and this does not mean caviar and truffles. Dogs need dog food, not people food.

Avoid any ingredients that may make your dog hyperactive, such as artificial colourings, sugars, wheat, milk and soya, and never, ever feed your dog chocolate. The first few listed can lead to behaviour problems, while chocolate can be fatal. See page 102 for more information.

GIVING YOU THE RUN AROUND

It's that old adage: start as you mean to go on. Once again, what applies to raising toddlers works well when dealing with dogs. It is vital that you set consistent boundaries from the outset. Don't wait for things to go wrong, as prevention is better (and easier) than cure. You can always relax the rules later on, when your dog has learnt its place within your household. Teach your dog to sit patiently at the front door (on the lead) before going out and also when greeting guests. This will prevent wild and uncontrolled behaviour later on. Dogs are often whipped up into a frenzy by their unwitting owners, only to be unfairly criticized for the resulting overexuberance (see pages 52–3).

CHILDREN AND DOGS

Always supervise young children when they are around dogs, and never leave the two alone together or turn your back on them – not even for a moment. This is especially true when it comes to puppies. Both children and puppies need to be taught how to behave around each other, so separate them if one is annoying the other (see page 37).

TRAVEL TROUBLES

Make sure your dog is comfortable and familiar with travelling quietly in the car. If you don't, it may become carsick or overexcited whenever you go on trips. Even if you aren't planning to take your dog on holidays or extended outings in the car, there will be times when you will need to resort to some sort of vehicular transport, such as on a trip to the vet's. It is best to make sure that this experience does not turn into a nightmare every time (see page 139).

Left Keep your dog off the furniture by giving it a bed of its own.

dog play like this with any item of clothing, old or otherwise, as it may not be able to differentiate between what is and isn't allowed to be chewed.

The dog can be allowed to win possession occasionally, as long as you win most of the time. Winning means that you decide when the game finishes as you end up with the toy and can put it away for a while. Your dog must not be allowed to growl at you (so don't growl at it, even if it is in play). If this does happen, stop the game immediately.

APPROPRIATE PLAY

Only play gentle games, as rough play will make your dog wild and aggressive, or suspicious and distrustful. Dogs become really confused and frustrated when they are encouraged to play rough, boisterous games one minute, then told off for it the next. Playful growling and play biting may appear harmless from a small puppy, but this often develops into serious behaviour when they grow older.

Any games that incite wrestling, teasing, growling, play biting, barking or hysterical behaviour should not be allowed. If your dog learns how to deflect you in play, it can use the same technique to manipulate you in real life. If it exhibits any of these behaviours, stop the game, then studiously ignore the dog for about ten minutes to communicate your disdain.

Channel any mouthing (play biting) off you and onto a toy. Give the dog loads of quality attention each time it happens to show interest in one of its toys.

TUG-OF-WAR GAMES

Gentle tug-of-war games can be allowed with appropriate toys, but never let your

RETRIEVE GAMES

Don't let your dog 'mug' you for the toy. Encouraging dogs to jump up or snatch toys out of your hand can cause lots of unnecessary problems. Always make the dog sit before you throw the toy, and develop the habit of throwing the toy in different directions to keep the dog guessing and retain its interest.

If the dog tries to run away with the toy, put the toy (or the dog) on a piece of string, so that you can maintain control and prevent your dog from giving you the run around.

When your dog brings the toy back to you, don't nag it into giving it up or try to grab the toy. Dogs certainly don't lack cunning, and yours will simply learn to stay just out of arm's reach or will clamp onto the toy even harder.

Give your dog lots of praise and make a fuss of it for coming back before you show any interest in the toy. Next hold its collar, and ignore it completely. Your dog will quickly grow bored and drop the toy. Make a big fuss of the dog, then throw the toy again. Your dog will soon learn that your hand in its collar is the signal to give the toy up.

Finish all 'interactive' games by putting the current toy away and giving the dog a chew toy instead. Keep the toys in a toy basket (not in its bed), and rotate the toys so that your dog doesn't become blasé about them.

Avoid playing games where you chase your dog at home or in the park (either to catch it or to get a toy from it). These games of tag teach it that it can outrun you, something than can backfire badly if you don't have reliable recall.

PLAYING FOOTBALL

Kicking a ball around and encouraging your dog to chase and wrestle it is an extremely ill-advised game, as it causes ankle chasing and biting. This becomes a serious problem if the dog progresses to chasing, tripping up and biting joggers, footballers and any children in the park who happen to be playing with a ball. It also puts the dogs at risk of severe injury, so is best avoided.

DESTRUCTIVE BEHAVIOUR

Dogs destroy forbidden items for a variety of reasons. Mostly, they do this because they are bored, frustrated, do not have appropriate toys or are looking for attention. Other dogs destroy as a result of being stressed.

Furnish your dog with some good toys, so that it always has something appropriate to play with (see pages 118–19). Tether its toys in one area to encourage it to settle and play or chew there. This should reduce the chances of it indiscriminately chewing elsewhere. Praise your dog when it plays there. If it leaves the toy, pick it up and flaunt your possession of it before putting it away to make the dog want it more next time.

Teach your dog to settle (see pages 79–81) where its toys are tied up, and you can later progress to tethering it there for very short periods while it is playing with the toy. Use this tactic at times when the dog needs to be controlled. This is a much better option than shutting it away in another room, which could only serve to make it frustrated and start chewing things or barking and scratching at the door. By keeping the dog in the same room, you are at least allowing it to become accustomed to all the stimuli, without being allowed to run wild.

Left Encourage your dog to play fetching games using suitable toys.

> **TITBIT**
> Don't teach your puppy to 'speak' or give a paw until it is at least a year old, otherwise, it will only scratch you or bark whenever it wants anything. First teach it the sit, down and settle, and only teach the speak or paw when the dog is fully grown.

FREQUENTLY ASKED QUESTIONS

12

Like life, the pleasures and rewards of owning a dog will inevitably have their ups and downs, and everyone will probably encounter a slight hiccup with their dog and its behaviour at some point in the relationship. The following are some of the most frequently asked questions that crop up when people have a dog of their own. Read through this chapter to see if any of them apply to you and your dog.

HOW CAN I STOP MY DOG GOING TO THE TOILET OVERNIGHT?

Always feed your dog at regular times – don't leave food down or overfeed – and take the dog outside at regular times. If it is going to the toilet overnight, keep a record of the times it uses its bowels. Change one of the meal times to see which bowel motion this affects, and adjust accordingly. Always accompany your dog to the garden or backyard so that you can reward it for going outside (see page 34).

WHY DOESN'T MY PUPPY GO TO THE TOILET DURING ITS WALK?

If your puppy always waits until you are home before urinating or defecating in the garden or indoors, it is simply because dogs are creatures of habit. They like to 'go' where they are used to going to the toilet (see pages 36–7).

MY PUPPY RUNS AROUND LIKE A LUNATIC, ESPECIALLY AFTER EATING. HAS IT GONE MAD OR IS IT HYPERACTIVE?

The answer is probably neither. Most puppies have a mad five minutes (or half hour) when they let off steam and show off. Just ignore this behaviour – it needs to do it. At all costs, however, don't join in, or your puppy will only indulge in this

behaviour more often. Still, it may well be worth avoiding foods that could make your dog hyperactive (see page 102).

HOW CAN I PREVENT MY PUPPY FROM CHASING AND BITING MY YOUNG CHILD OR TODDLER?

Children and dogs easily misunderstand each other's signals. This particular type of behaviour arises because toddlers and young children often unwittingly attract it, so you should only let them interact with the dog under your supervision. Both dog and child need to be taught how to be gentle with each other. Keep them apart (use a child gate or playpen) if one or the other is having an exuberant moment, and never leave them alone together.

Left All puppies need an outlet for their excess energy and so exercise themselves by running around like lunatics for short periods.

Below Teach your dog to sit when greeted, to prevent any problems with jumping up on people.

HOW DO I PUT A STOP TO MY PUPPY PLAY BITING AND 'DIVE BOMBING' ME?

You need to make sure that you are not overexciting your dog with rough play or by touching it inappropriately. The majority of puppies – and, of course, fully grown dogs – actively dislike being patted or stroked on the head. Far from being soothing, it in fact makes them 'mouthy', as does vigorous rubbing. Dogs prefer to be stroked and scratched slowly and gently under the chin, on the neck and chest, behind the ears and along the back, especially just above the tail. Avoid the top of its head and around its face.

To overcome the problem of play biting and 'dive bombing', teach your puppy the settle exercise (see pages 79–81), then you can tether it to something secure with a chew toy whenever it is misbehaving. However, shutting it outside is not the solution. It will become frustrated, and won't learn anything constructive.

HOW DO I STOP MY DOG FROM JUMPING UP ON PEOPLE? I'M NOW TOO AFRAID TO LET HIM OFF THE LEAD IN THE PARK.

Start by teaching your dog to sit 100 percent of the time when greeting the family and guests at home (see page 52). This should make it much better mannered when you are out and about. Until the dog is reliable, you could exercise it on a long trailing line (see page 62). This will help you to control it, but remember that you still need to allow it to exercise and socialize properly with other dogs.

WHY DOES MY DOG URINATE WHEN I GREET IT?

This is not necessarily incontinence – it can be to do with overexcitement and submission. Your dog is overwhelmed and, as a result, acts submissively. Don't punish your dog for this behaviour, as the stress will make the problem worse. Delay your greeting until you can get the dog outdoors, and tone down the excitement, keeping it calm and short. This behaviour is more common with bitches and often disappears after the first season, so don't spay her before then (see page 94).

MY DOG IS NOT VERY GOOD WITH OTHER DOGS. CAN I DO ANYTHING ABOUT IT?

The answer to this question is not so simple, as this problem depends on many factors. Ask your vet to recommend a good dog trainer or behaviour therapist, who will take all the factors into consideration and give you an informed opinion.

time and learn how to do it yourself, or don't have a dog. If you don't have time for training, then you certainly don't have time for the commitment of dog ownership.

MY DOG IS A FUSSY EATER AND PREFERS OUR FOOD. SHOULD I GIVE IT MORE VARIETY OR COOK SPECIALLY FOR IT?

Neither of these is the answer. Most owners routinely overfeed commercial dog food and worry when the dog eats less than the recommended amount. Chopping and changing diets will simply make it fussier and could cause food intolerances. See pages 98–104 for strategies on diet.

WHY DOES MY DOG EAT ITS FAECES?

This could be due to a number of reasons: illness, worms, inappropriate diet, poor digestion, attention-seeking behaviour, boredom, guilt, over- or underfeeding, poor living conditions, or bad habits learnt in the nest (commonly seen in dogs bred at puppy farms or dogs from pet stores). Some breeds are more prone to do this than others. Ask your vet for advice.

I AM FRIGHTENED OF OTHER PEOPLE'S DOGS AND FEARFUL OF TAKING MY DOG TO THE PARK IN CASE WE MEET SOME. WHAT SHOULD I DO?

Your dog needs to mix with other dogs (see page 41), so you will simply have to overcome your fears. If you exercise your dog at popular dog walking times, most of the dogs you will meet will be fine, as the owners of aggressive dogs tend to avoid the crowds. A good dog-training club will help you overcome your trepidation – in the meantime, ask someone else to walk your dog for you.

HOW CAN I STOP MY DOG FROM PULLING ON THE LEAD?

Quite simply, train it not to, or use a training aid (see pages 74–5).

I'M A VERY BUSY PERSON. SHOULD I SEND MY DOG AWAY FOR TRAINING?

No! Residential dog training can be very harsh and sometimes cruel, and you won't find out until it is too late. Even if you are lucky and find a kind trainer, if you haven't learnt how to reinforce your dog's training, it will quickly break down and the dog will revert to its previous behaviour. Find the

MY DOG BARKS AT THE DOOR BELL. SHOULD I STOP IT?

As long as your dog stops barking when told, it should be fine. The problems start when the dog won't stop barking because it is too hyped up, so make sure that you stay in control to prevent this happening.

I'M FRIGHTENED TO LET MY DOG OFF THE LEAD. DOES IT REALLY NEED TO RUN FREE?

Yes! All dogs need proper exercise, with free running and mixing with their own species, or they will grow frustrated and develop behaviour and training problems. Teach a reliable recall, using a long line if necessary (see page 49), and enrol your dog at a good dog-training class if it is easily distracted.

SHOULD I TIE MY DOG OUTSIDE A STORE WHILE I'M SHOPPING?

It's better not to, as they are frequently compromised by other dogs or children. As they can't get away, they often snap or bite, and it is unfair for them to be held responsible for this. They could also be stolen, so don't take the risk.

SHOULD I NEUTER MY DOG?

The evidence suggests that neutered dogs are both healthier and happier. Unless you have a particular reason for keeping your dog 'intact' (for example, if you are going to show or breed your dog), it is probably best to neuter it at the appropriate age. See pages 93–7 for advice on when to neuter and the pros and cons of doing so.

WILL HAVING MY DOG CASTRATED TAKE AWAY HIS PERSONALITY?

Absolutely not. You don't need a pair of testicles to have personality – just ask any woman. In fact, castration often improves a dog's temperament, so it can only be wholeheartedly recommended.

MY CIRCUMSTANCES HAVE CHANGED, AND I NEED TO GO TO WORK ALL DAY. HOW LONG CAN I LEAVE MY DOG ALONE, AND SHOULD I GET ANOTHER DOG TO KEEP IT COMPANY?

Don't get another dog just for company, as most dogs would rather have their owners to themselves and resent the competition, especially if their shared time is reduced. Also, why subject two dogs to a boring day, instead of just one? Most adult dogs are normally fine on their own for four-hour

Left All dogs need to be able to run around freely as part of their daily exercise regime.

stretches, as long as someone takes them out to answer the call of nature and stretch their legs around midday. If you can't find a neighbour or friend to look after your dog or take it out, employ a reputable dog walker or minder. Choose carefully, as some are good and some are awful.

MY DOG IS DRAGGING ITS BOTTOM ALONG THE GROUND. DOES THIS MEAN IT HAS WORMS?

Not necessarily. It means it has an itchy bottom, and the most common cause of this is anal gland problems. Take your dog to your vet for diagnosis and treatment.

HOW DO I FIND A GOOD KENNEL?

Go by recommendation only. Ask your vet, dog trainer and other dog walkers. Visit the kennels first, and take your dog for a trial overnight stay to ensure it is happy there. You can then go and enjoy your holiday without feeling so worried about your dog.

HOW CAN I CALM MY DOG'S FEAR OF THUNDER AND FIREWORKS?

Frightened dogs like to hide in small, dark places, so give yours a safe haven, with a towel or an old jumper for comfort. Keep your dog inside, as frightened dogs have been known to escape out of 'safe' gardens, open windows, doors and cars. Close all your windows and curtains, turn up the radio or television, and act in an upbeat manner. Try not to fuss over your dog unduly, as this may make it worse. Homeopathic remedies or sedatives from the vet may also give some relief.

If you do have to take your dog out when there is thunder nearby, keep it on a lead or strong long line in case it panics and runs away. Ensure that it is wearing an identity disc with all your details, is microchipped and is fully insured.

MY DOG HAS TRIED TO BITE SOMEONE. SHOULD I MUZZLE IT?

Seek professional help immediately. Ask your vet to recommend a reputable dog behaviour therapist, and muzzle your dog in the meantime if you are unsure of its temperament when in public.

WHAT IF I WANT TO TAKE MY DOG ABROAD?

If you intend to travel to another country with your dog, you should ask your vet about the rules and regulations well in advance of travelling. You need to allow adequate time to fulfil any requirements such as a quarantine period.

WHY DOES MY DOG STEAL UNDERWEAR, SHOES, SLIPPERS AND PENS?

For attention (see pages 49–52).

Left Your dog may seem happy to lie around all day, but it does need to be taken out every few hours.

Left Stealing and chewing an item of clothing or footwear is often a plea for attention.

DO I NEED TO TAKE ANY SPECIAL CARE WITH MY DOG IN THE CAR?

Absolutely. Travelling in a car is not a natural activity for a dog and it may take a while for them to get used to it. Here are some precautions you should take:

Don't feed your dog prior to travelling, as this may make it carsick.

Don't allow your dog to hang its head out of an open window, as this is very dangerous. At worst, it could fall or jump out, but there is the ever-present threat of eye infections, too.

Your dog should always be tethered to something secure, to prevent it running amok or perhaps wheedling its way into the front seat, where it can all too easily interfere with the driver or get hurt (or run away) in the event of an accident.

A car harness that attaches to a car seat belt or luggage lashing point will keep your dog safer than a conventional dog guard should the worst happen and the windows break during a crash. This type of harness also prevents the dog jumping out prematurely when the door is opened. Keep the tether short to prevent the dog becoming tangled up and hurting itself. Alternatively, you could use a travelling crate. Bear in mind that tethering your dog with its collar and lead is better than nothing at all. Always untie your dog and take off its lead and harness when you are leaving it in the car.

Don't ever let your dog get too warm in the car. If you have to travel on a sunny day, use sun blinds (or newspaper and sticky tape in an emergency) for the side windows. This will protect the dog from

overheating in its fur coat. Dogs do not perspire as we do, so circulating air does not cool them as effectively as it does humans, and an open window does not provide a dog with any protection from the heating effect of the sun.

Never leave your dog in a car on a sunny (or even overcast but warm) day, even with the windows partially open. The glass windows act like a greenhouse and the metal roof like a radiator. Even on an overcast day, it can still become warm enough inside a car to kill a dog.

Heat stroke can kill a dog in minutes, and many dogs become ill and die each year unnecessarily because their owners naively thought them to be safe. If you see a dog in a car on a warm day, call the police to take remedial action, as these dog owners are breaking the law and gambling with their dog's life.

Always carry a bottle of water and a bowl in the car to offer your dog drinks regularly during journeys. Also keep a hand towel that can be soaked to wet the dog down – or dry the dog off – and always have your vet's phone number to hand in the car, in case of an emergency.

ADDRESS BOOK

ORGANIZATIONS IN THE UK

Barnet and Mill Hill District
Dog Training Clubs
50 Tudor Road
Barnet, Herts EN5 5NP
Tel: 020 8449 7539
or 020 8959 0055
www.trainingdogs.co.uk
The organization offers dog
training and care classes in
North London.

**Battersea Dogs
and Cats Home**
4 Battersea Park Road
London SW8 4AA
Tel: 020 7622 3626
www.dogshome.org
The Home runs two rehoming
centres for London's stray
and lost dogs and cats.

Blue Cross Adoption Centre
Shilton Road
Burford
Oxon OX18 4PF
Tel: 01993 822651
www.bluecross.org.uk
The Blue Cross has several
rehoming centres for dogs
and cats nationally.

The Cinnamon Trust
10 Market Square
Hayle
Cornwall TR27 4HE
Tel: 01736 757900
www.cinnamon.org.uk
The Trust works to help the
elderly and terminally ill
with their pets and offers a
national fostering service.

The Kennel Club
1 Clarges Street
London W1J 8AB
Tel: 0870 606 6750
www.the-kennel-club.org.uk
The Kennel Club has details
of 'breed clubs' and 'breed
rescue societies' who can
tell you about the breed and
common problems, and help
find a responsible breeder or
rehome a dog.

Mayhew Animal Home
Trenmar Garden
Kensal Green
London NW10 6BJ
Tel: 020 8969 0178
www.mayhewanimalhome.org
Rehoming centre for dogs
and other small animals.

**National Canine Defence
League (NCDL)**
17 Wakley Street
London EC1V 7RQ
Tel: 020 7837 0006
www.ncdl.org.uk
NCDL has several rehoming
centres throughout the UK.

**People's Dispensary for
Sick Animals (PDSA)**
Whitechapel Way
Priorslee
Telford
Shropshire TF2 9PQ
Tel: 01952 290999
www.pdsa.org.uk
A charity that helps with
veterinary care for sick and
injured pets of needy people.

**Royal Society for the
Prevention of Cruelty
to Animals (RSPCA)**
Wilberforce Way
Southwater, Horsham
West Sussex
Helpline: 0870 555 5999
www.rspca.org.uk
The RSPCA has rehoming
centres for dogs and other
animals nationally.

**Scottish Society for the
Prevention of Cruelty to
Animals (SSPCA)**
Kingseat Road, Halbeath
Dunfermline KY11 8RY
Helpline: 03000 999 999
www.scottishspca.org
Scottish rehoming centres for
dogs and other animals.

ORGANIZATIONS IN THE USA

American Kennel Club (AKC)
8051 Arco Corporate Drive
Suite 100
Raleigh, NC 27617-3390
Telephone: 919 233 9767
www.akc.org
The club keeps a register of
purebred dogs and offers
breeder referral and
professional dog training.

**American Society for the
Prevention of Cruelty to
Animals (ASPCA)**
424 East 92nd Street
New York, NY 10128
Tel: 212 876 7700
www.aspca.org
Runs rehoming centres for
dogs and other animals.

PET ACCESSORY & CARE : UK

The Barking Bedgebury
(dog hotel)
www.bestdoghotel.co.uk

Canine Country Club
(dog hotel)
Morton Folly
Youlstone
Bude
Cornwall EX23 9PT
Tel: 01288 331216
www.caninecountryclub.co.uk

Diva Dogs Pet Boutique
and Grooming Parlour
42 New Street
Chelmsford
Essex CM1 1PH
Tel: 01245 49 66 44
www.divadogs.co.uk

Doggie Style Store
www.doggiestylestore.com

Grand Union Pets
174 Shirland Road
Maida Vale
London W9 3JE
Tel: 020 7289 5375
www.grandunionpets.co.uk

Kyra and Luna's
Pet Boutique
www.kyraandluna.co.uk

Little Scruffs Pet Boutique
www.littlescruffs.com

Max and Margot Dog
Company
www.maxandmargot.co.uk

Mungo & Maud
www.mungoandmaud.com

The Mutz Nutz
221 Westbourne Park Road
London W11 1EA
Tel: 020 7243 3333
www.themutznutz.com

Pet Pavilion
Chelsea Farmers Market
125 Sydney Street
London SW3 6NR
Tel: 020 7376 8800
www.petpavillion.co.uk
Stockists of exclusive
accessories to suit every pet
lover's tastes and budget.

Petcrazee
www.petzcrazee.com

Posh Dogz & Co
Mains of Gight Cottage
Methlick
Aberdeenshire, AB41 7HY
Tel: 01651806718
www.poshdogz.co.uk

Waggin Tails Pet Boutique
and Grooming Spa
366 Fulham Road
London, SW10 9UU
Tel: 0207 823 3111
www.waggintailsonline.com

Ritz Canine Luxury
Dog Resort
Whitecroft
Collets Green
Worcester WR2 4RY
Tel: 01905 830 380
www.ritz-canine.com

PET ACCESSORY & CARE :
USA

Dogbedworks
Tel: 413 296 0363
www.dogbedworks.com
Stocks stylish dog beds,
crates, ramps, furniture
and travel gear.

Happy Paws
www.happypawsdaycare.com

Paw Palace Online
www.pawpalaceonline.com

Running Paws
www.runningpaws.com

Tails in the City
One East Delaware Place
Chicago, IL 60611
Tel: 1-312-649-0347
www.tailsinthecity.com

The Yuppy Puppy
8104 Main Street
Ellicott City
MD 21043
Tel: 410 750 9663
www.theyuppypuppy
petboutique.com

Ruff Wear
Tel: 541 388 1821
or 888 783 3932
www.ruffwear.com
Dog clothes, accessories and
toys available via the Internet
or mail order, or phone for
your nearest stockist.

INDEX

ACKNOWLEDGEMENTS

Page 1 Carlton Books, Page 2 Courtesy Burberry, Page 3 Carlton Books, Page 4–5 Conde Nast syndication, Page 6 Courtesy Cath Kidston, Page 10 Bobbie Courtesy Tamsin Foster, Page 11 The Image Bank/Getty Images, Page 12 Tony Stone/Getty Images, Page14 Tony Stone/Getty Images, Page 15 Tony Stone/Getty Images, Page 16T RSPCA Photo Library, 16R The Image Bank/Getty Images, 16B Bobbie Courtesy Tamsin Foster, 16L The Image Bank/Getty Images, Page 17 Corbis, Page 18 The Image Bank/Getty Images, Page 19 The Image Bank/Getty Images, Page 20 Tony Stone/Getty Images, Page 21 Tony Stone/Getty Images, Page 22 Photodisc, Page 23 Eyewire, Page 24 The Image Bank/Getty Images, Page 25 Tony Stone/Getty Images, Page 26 Superstock, Page 27 Sally Anne Thompson Animal Photography, Page 28 FPAGE/Getty Images, Page 29 The Image Bank/Getty Images, Page 30 Carlton Books, Page 31 Tony Stone/Getty Images, Page 32 The Image Bank/Getty Images, Page 33 The Image Bank/Getty Images, Page 35 FPAGE/Getty Images, Page 36 The Image Bank/Getty Images, Page 39 FPAGE/Getty Images, Page 40 FPAGE/Getty Images, Page 41 Photonica, Page 42 Tony Stone/Getty Images, Page 43 The Image Bank/Getty Images, Page 45 The Image Bank/Getty Images, Page 46 Tony Stone/Getty Images, Page 47 The Image Bank/Getty Images, Page 48 Tony Stone/Getty Images, Page 50 FPAGE/Getty Images, Page 51T FPAGE/Getty Images, 51B Photodisc, Page 53 Tony Stone/Getty Images, Page 55 Tony Stone/Getty Images, Page 56 Carlton Books, Page 57 Carlton Books, Page 58 Carlton Books, Page 59 Carlton Books, Page 60 Carlton Books, Page 61 Carlton Books, Page 63 FPAGE/Getty Images, Page 64 Carlton Books, Page 65 Carlton Books, Page 66 Carlton Books, Page 67 Carlton Books, Page 68 Carlton Books, Page 69 Carlton Books, Page 70 The Image Bank/Getty Images, Page 71 RSPCA Photo Library, Page 72 FPAGE/Getty Images, Page 73 Photodisc, Page 74 Tony Stone/Getty Images, Page 75 Carlton Books, Page 76 RSPCA Photo Library, Page 77 The Image Bank/Getty Images, Page 78 FPAGE/Getty Images, Page 79 RSPCA Photo Library, Page 80 Carlton Books, Page 81 Carlton Books, Page 82 Courtesy Burberry, Page 83 Seamus Ryan Courtesy of Virgin Atlantic, Page 84 The Image Bank/Getty Images, Page 85 Tony Stone/Getty Images, Page 86 FPAGE/Getty Images, Page 87 Carlton Books, Page 88 The Image Bank/Getty Images, Page 89 Tony Stone/Getty Images, Page 90 FPAGE/Getty Images, Page 91 The Image Bank/Getty Images, Page 92T Tony Stone/Getty Images, 92B Carlton Books, Page 95T Photodisc, 95B Tony Stone/Getty Images, Page 96 FPAGE/Getty Images, Page 97 FPAGE/Getty Images, Page 98 FPAGE/Getty Images, Page 99 RSPCA Photo Library, Page 100 The Image Bank/Getty Images, Page 101 RSPCA Photo Library, Page 102 Carlton Books, Page 103T FPAGE/Getty Images, 102B RSPCA Photo Library, Page 104 ImageState, Page 105 Carlton Books, Page 106 ImageState, Page 107 The Image Bank/Getty Images, Page 108L Carlton Books, 108R Robert Harding, Page 109 Carlton Books, Page 110 Photonica, Page 111T Courtesy Kong, 111B Carlton Books, Page 112 RSPCA Photo Library, Page 113L The Image Bank/Getty Images, 113R The Image Bank/Getty Images, Page114 Courtesy Browns Focus, Page 115 Carlton Books, Page 116 RSPCA Photo Library, Conde Nast Syndication, Page 117 Conde Nast Syndication, Page 118 Courtesy Kong, Page 119 Carlton Books, Page120TR Conde Nast Syndication, 120BL Batzi Co., Page 121 FPAGE/Getty Images, Page 122 Carlton Books, Page 123TL Carlton Books, 123TC Courtesy Woof Woof, 123CL Courtesy Woof Woof, 123C Courtesy Browns Focus, 123CR Courtesy Woof Woof, 123BL FPAGE/Getty Images, 123BL Courtesy Woof Woof, 123BC Courtesy Woof Woof, 123BR Carlton Books, Page 124 The Image Bank/Getty Images, Page 125 The Image Bank/Getty Images, Page 126 FPAGE/Getty Images, Page 127 Tony Stone/Getty Images, Page 129 Tony Stone/Getty Images, Page 130 Tony Stone/Getty Images, Page 131 The Image Bank/Getty Images, Page 132 FPAGE/Getty Images, Page 133 The Image Bank/Getty Images, Page 134 FPAGE/Getty Images, Page 135 The Image Bank/Getty Images, Page 136 Photonica, Page 137 FPAGE/Getty Images, Page 138 The Image Bank/Getty Images, Page 139 Sally Anne Thompson Animal Photography, Page 144 Carlton Books.

Author's Acknowledgements:

Many dogs and people have contributed to my knowledge over the years. Bebe, Pepper, Purdey, Eenie, Bundle, Monty, Kayleigh and Jasper were all unique animals who taught me different lessons, and none of this would have been possible had it not been for the humour, patience and friendship of my co-trainers Shirley Paine and Kevin McNicholas.

I am also massively grateful to the other talented trainers who have shared their knowledge and friendship with me over the years, including Sylvia Bishop, Binnie Iggulden, John Rogerson, Dot and Ian Watts, Jackie Mumford and Sandy Wadhams.

Friends and colleagues Alyson Young, Viv Stanton, Fiona Pinder MRCVS, and Linda and Richard Leonard MRCVS originally encouraged me to pursue a career in dog training and behaviour therapy. I am also indebted to Robert Harlow of The Kennel Club, Lyn Owen of the Guide Dogs for the Blind Association, Inspector Keith MacKenzie, Chief Instructor at the Metropolitan Police Dog Training Establishment, Billie MacQueen and Maddy Darrall from Disney TV and Darrall MacQueen Productions, and Liz Thornton from A1 Animals for encouraging me to extend my skills.

I would also like to thank Carlton for asking me to write this book; Zia Mattocks for her patience; Michelle Hurst and her two lovely pointers, Alfie and Tess; the Rose family; and Walt Disney Productions for allowing Jasper to appear in the book. Thanks also to my best friend Dr Julie Taylor-Browne for her tireless support and help with editing this book.

Finally, I am grateful to my mother Lisa and my sister Sue, whose long-suffering yet constant support have inspired and allowed me to follow my dreams.

This book is dedicated to the memory of my late father S. Kaye Conn, a unique man who led an extraordinary life.